JAZZ PIANO SOLOS VOLUME 26

george gershwin

Arranged by Brent Edstrom

contents

2 BIDIN' MY TIME

6 BUT NOT FOR ME

10 EMBRACEABLE YOU

14 FASCINATING RHYTHM

18 A FOGGY DAY (IN LONDON TOWN)

26 HOW LONG HAS THIS BEEN GOING ON?

21 I GOT PLENTY O' NUTTIN'

30 I GOT RHYTHM

40 I LOVES YOU, PORGY

44 I'VE GOT A CRUSH ON YOU

48 IT AIN'T NECESSARILY SO

35 LET'S CALL THE WHOLE THING OFF

52 LOVE IS HERE TO STAY

56 LOVE WALKED IN

60 THE MAN I LOVE

64 NICE WORK IF YOU CAN GET IT

74 OH, LADY BE GOOD!

78 'S WONDERFUL

69 SOMEBODY LOVES ME

82 SOMEONE TO WATCH OVER ME

87 SUMMERTIME

94 THEY ALL LAUGHED

90 THEY CAN'T TAKE THAT AWAY FROM ME

Cover photo © Alamy

ISBN 978-1-4768-1847-4

Visit Hal Leonard Online at
www.halleonard.com

Contact us:
Hal Leonard
7777 West Bluemound Road
Milwaukee, WI 53213
Email: info@halleonard.com

In Europe, contact:
Hal Leonard Europe Limited
42 Wigmore Street
Marylebone, London, W1U 2RN
Email: info@halleonardeurope.com

In Australia, contact:
Hal Leonard Australia Pty. Ltd.
4 Lentara Court
Cheltenham, Victoria, 3192 Australia
Email: info@halleonard.com.au

BIDIN' MY TIME

Music and Lyrics by GEORGE GERSHWIN
and IRA GERSHWIN

Moderate Swing

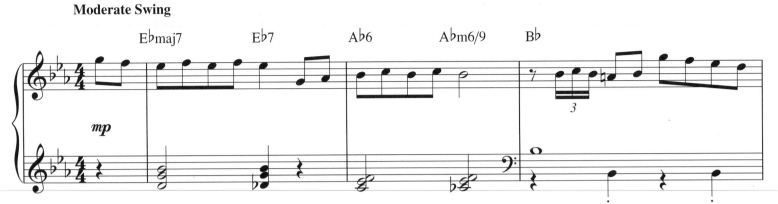

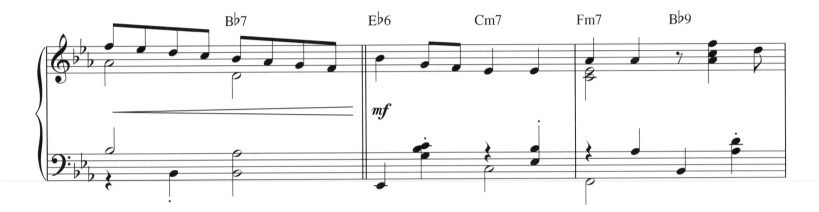

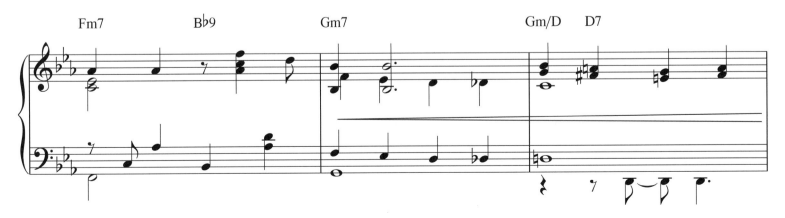

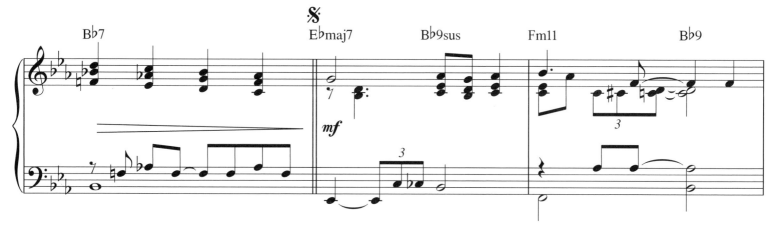

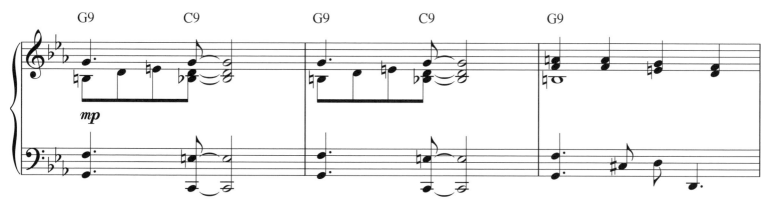

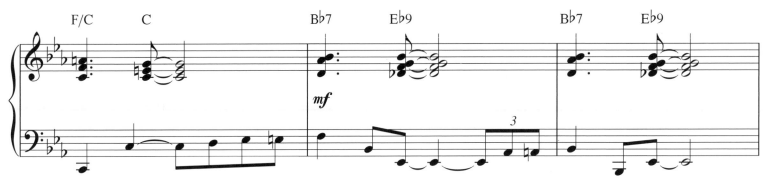

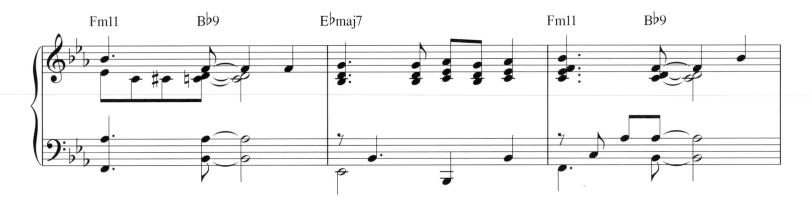

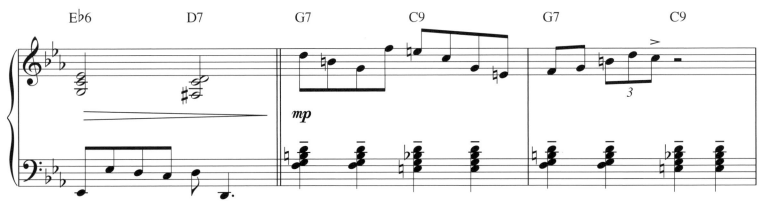

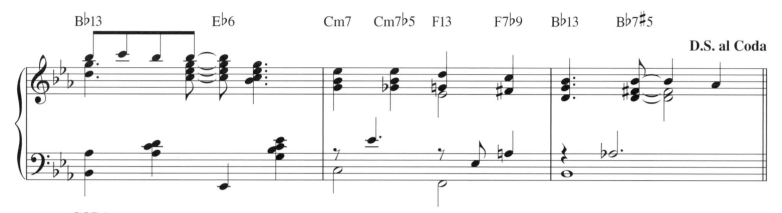

D.S. al Coda

CODA

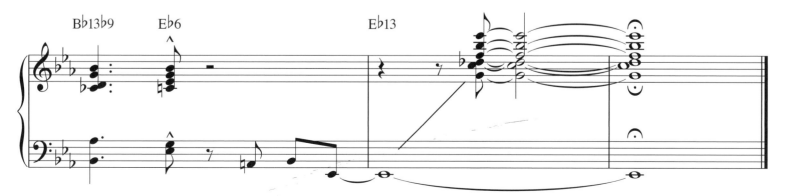

BUT NOT FOR ME

Music and Lyrics by GEORGE GERSHWIN
and IRA GERSHWIN

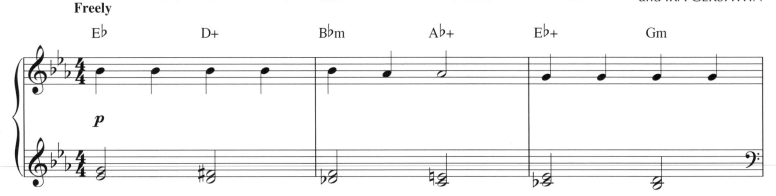

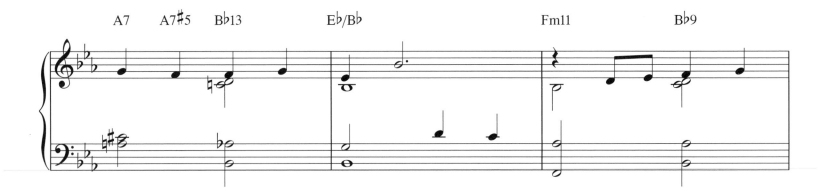

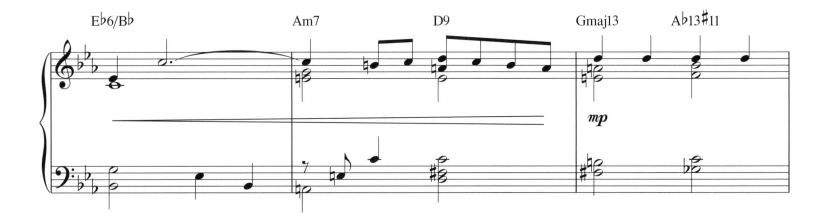

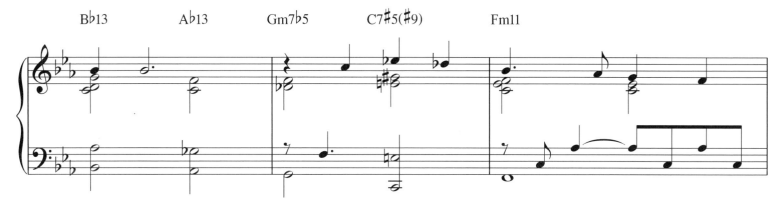

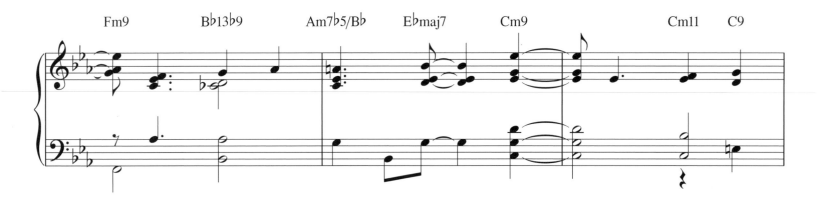

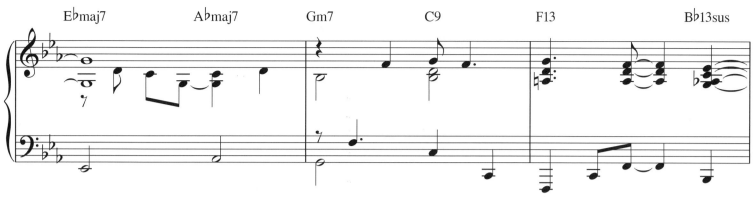

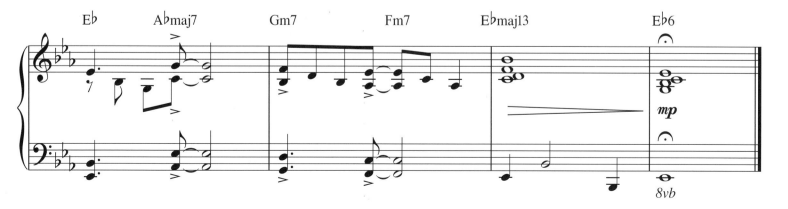

EMBRACEABLE YOU
from CRAZY FOR YOU

Music and Lyrics by GEORGE GERSHWIN
and IRA GERSHWIN

Whimsically

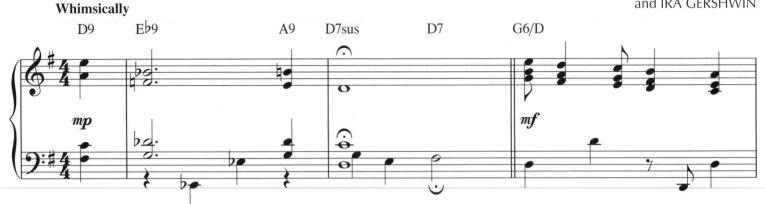

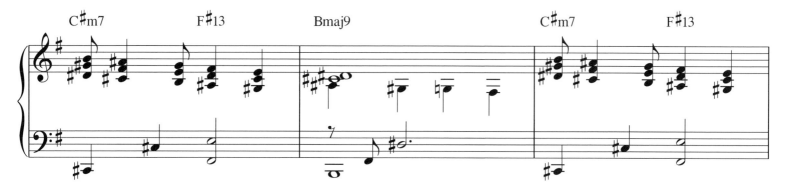

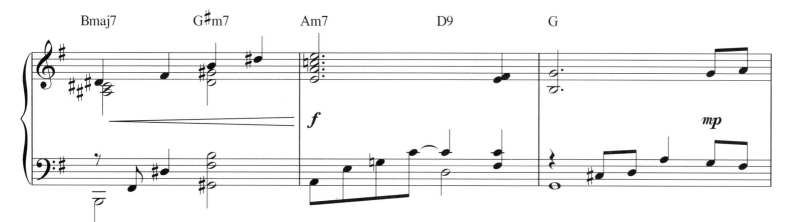

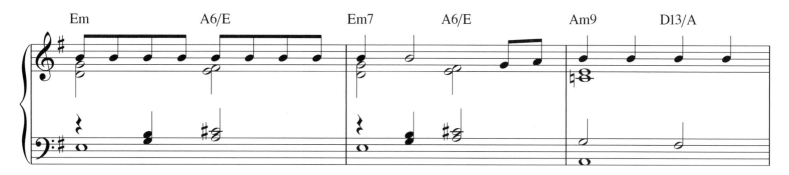

Steady Ballad tempo

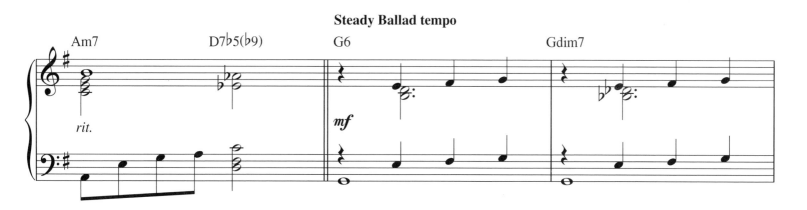

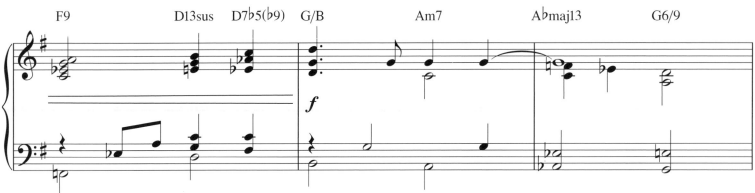

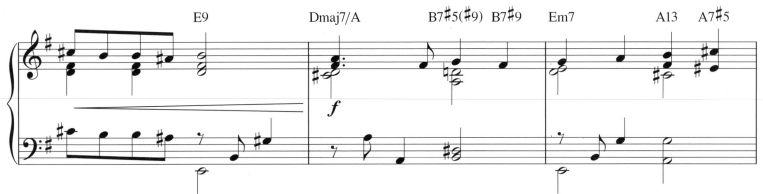

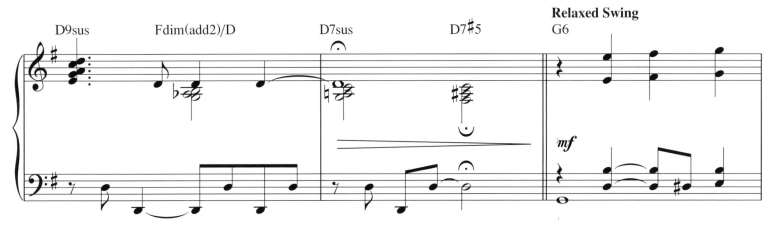

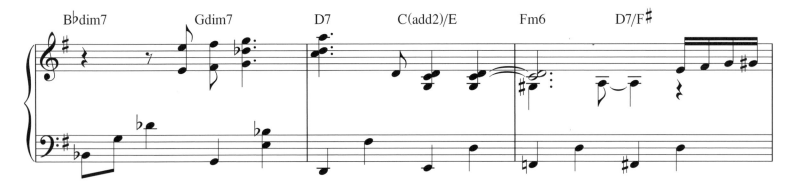

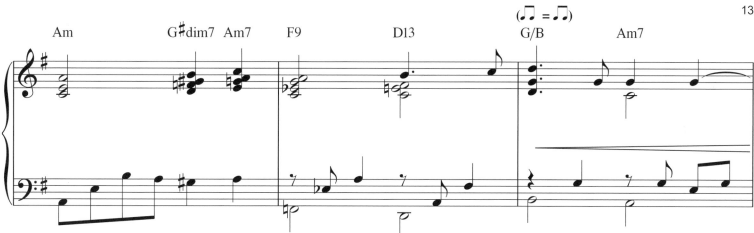

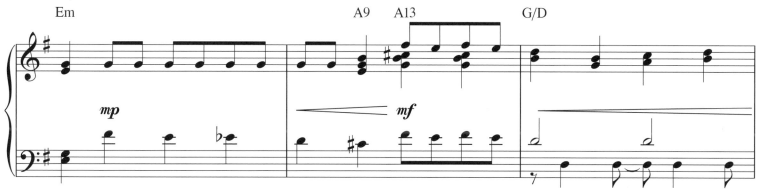

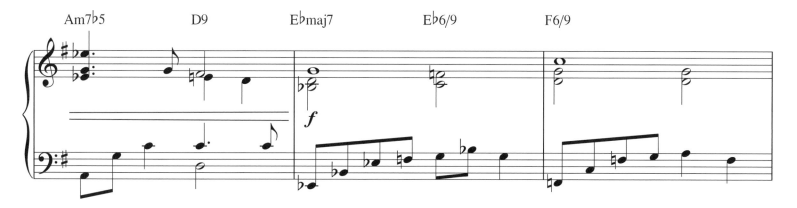

FASCINATING RHYTHM

Music and Lyrics by GEORGE GERSHWIN
and IRA GERSHWIN

Slowly, with rubato

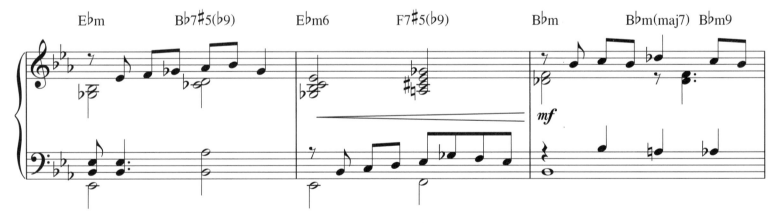

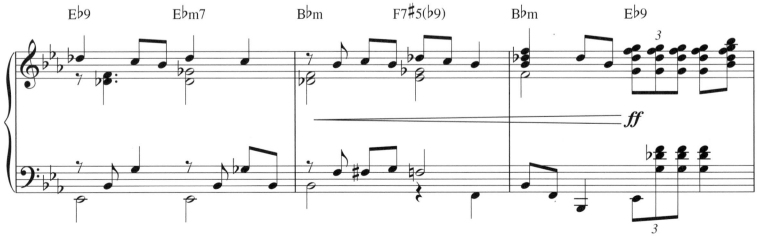

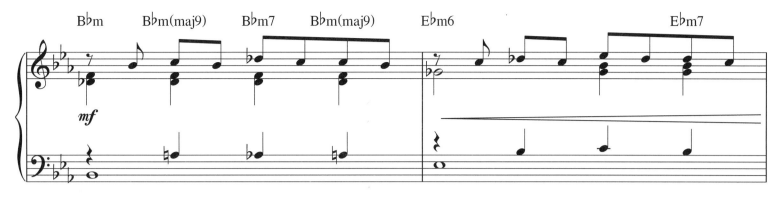

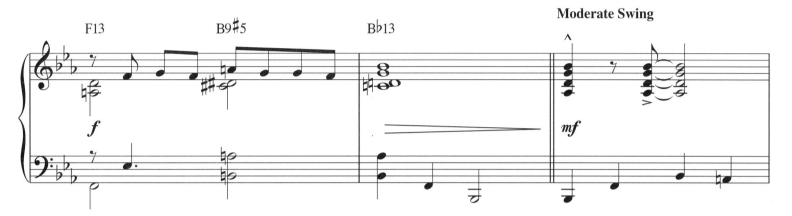

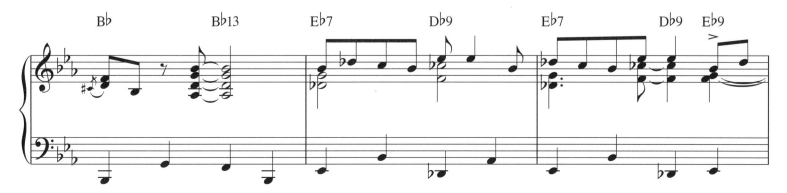

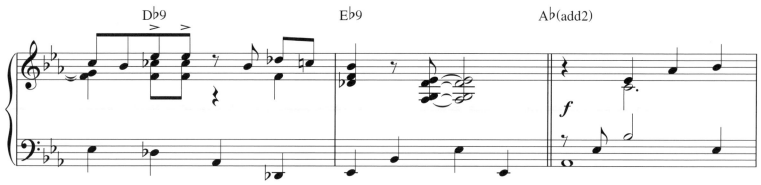

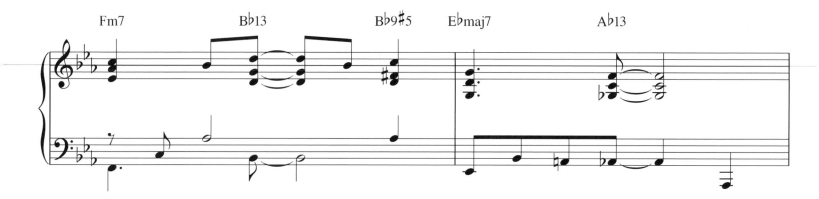

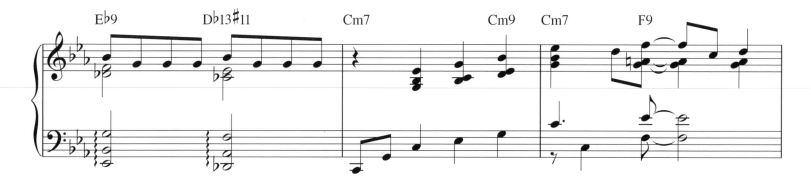

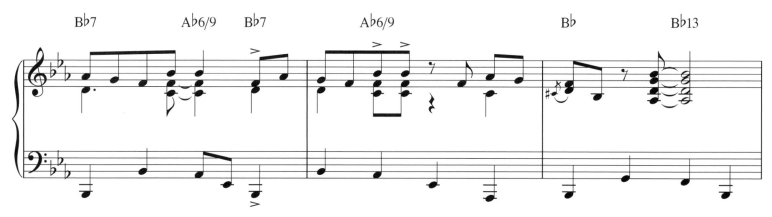

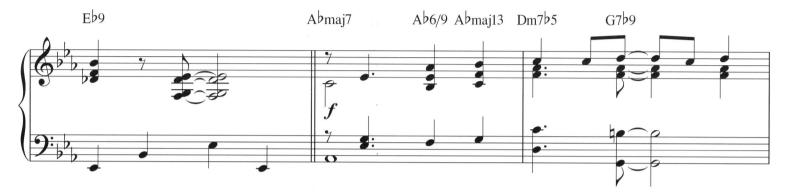

A FOGGY DAY
(In London Town)

Music and Lyrics by GEORGE GERSHWIN
and IRA GERSHWIN

Moderate Swing

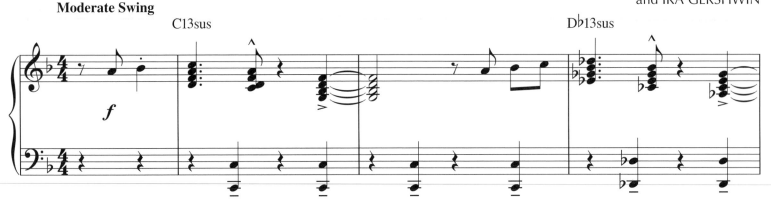

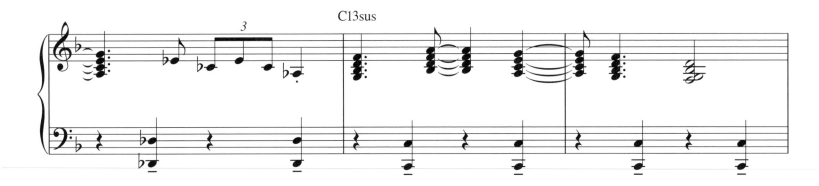

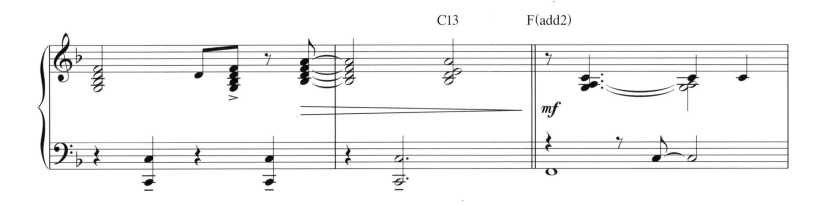

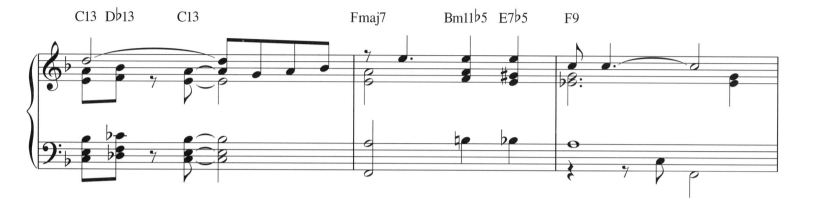

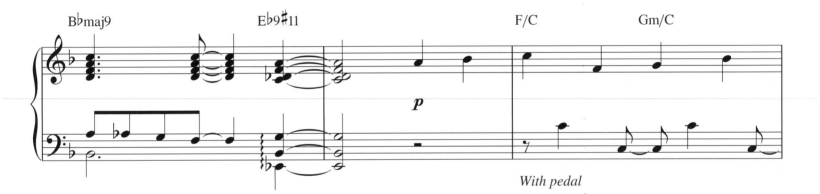

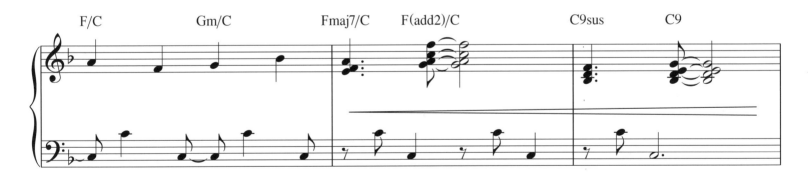

I GOT PLENTY O' NUTTIN'

from PORGY AND BESS®

Music and Lyrics by GEORGE GERSHWIN,
DU BOSE and DOROTHY HEYWARD
and IRA GERSHWIN

Medium Swing

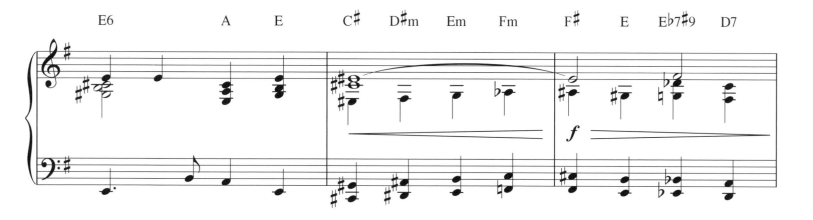

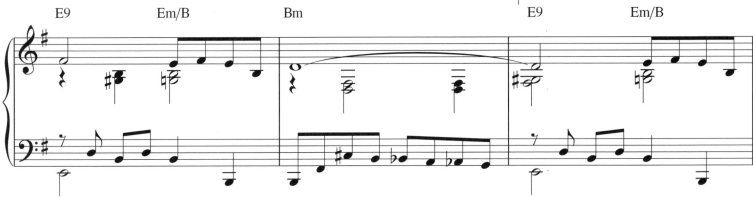

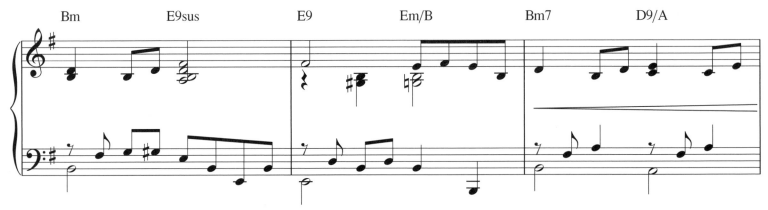

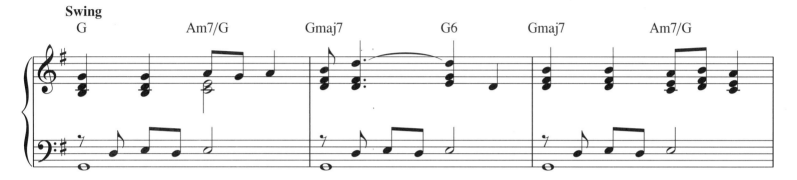

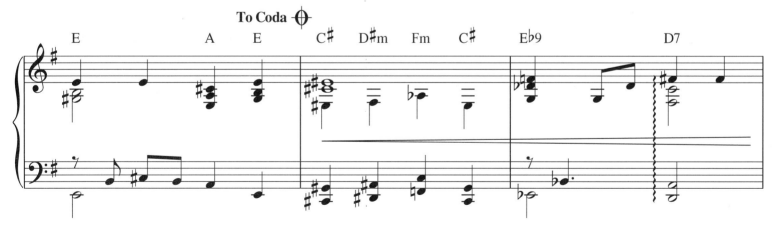

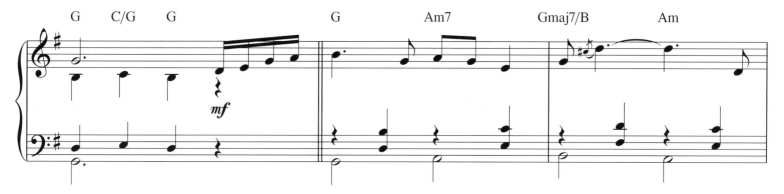

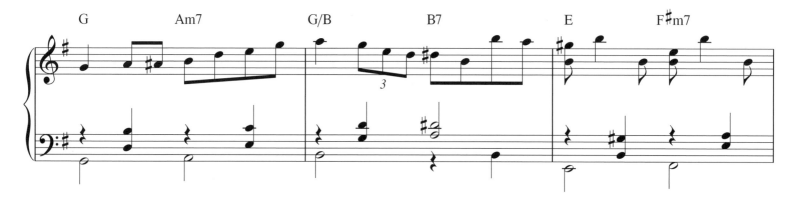

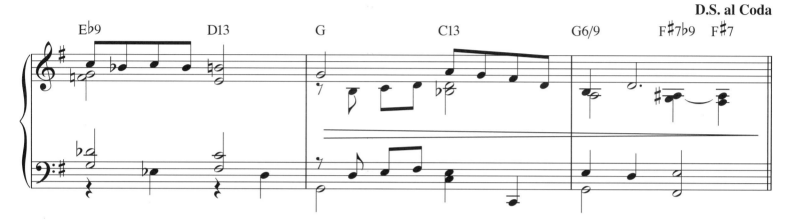

D.S. al Coda

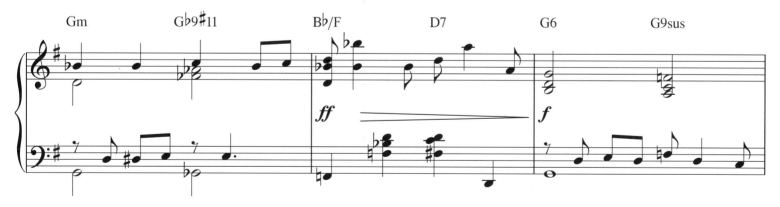

HOW LONG HAS THIS BEEN GOING ON?

Music and Lyrics by GEORGE GERSWIN
and IRA GERSHWIN

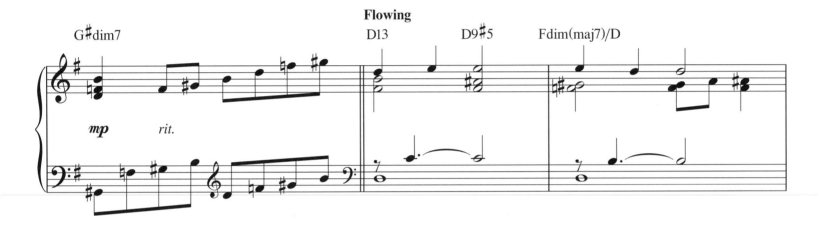

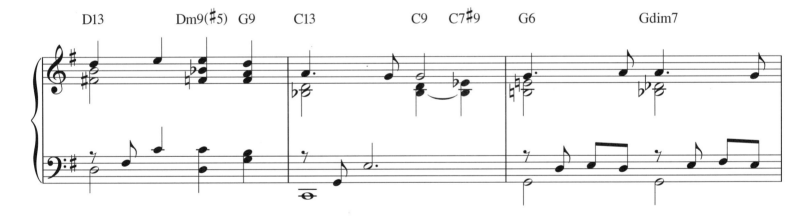

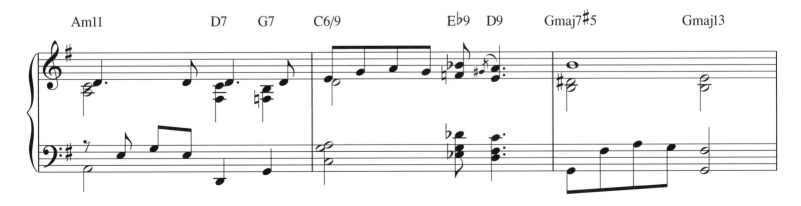

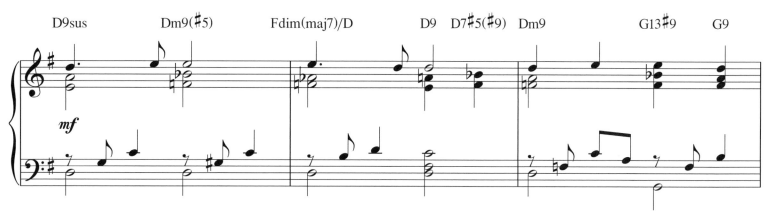
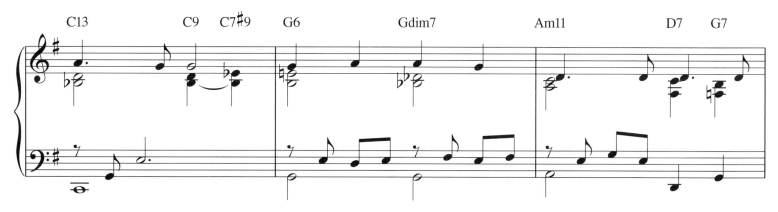
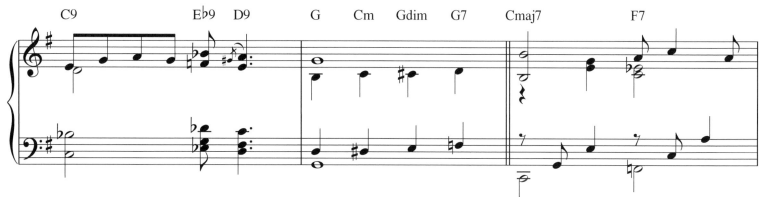
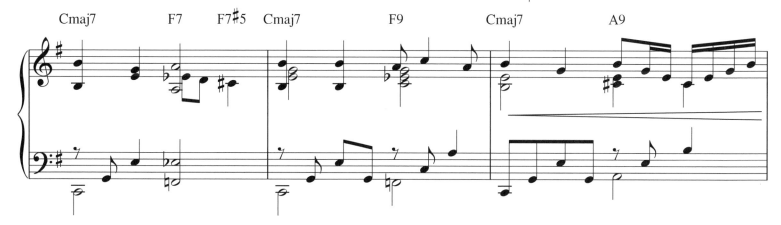

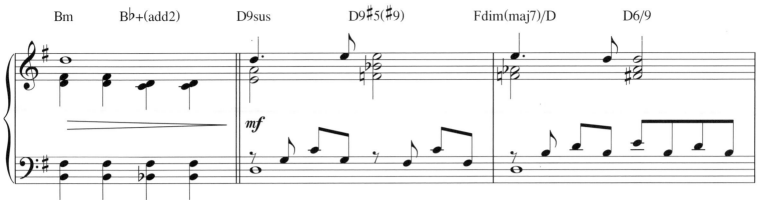

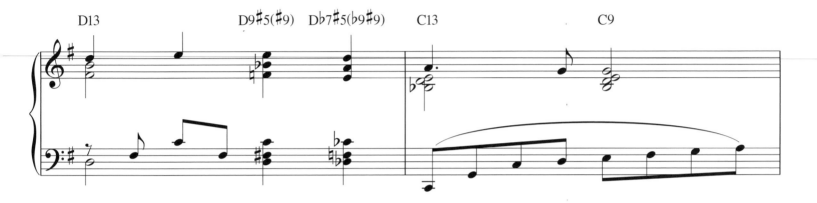

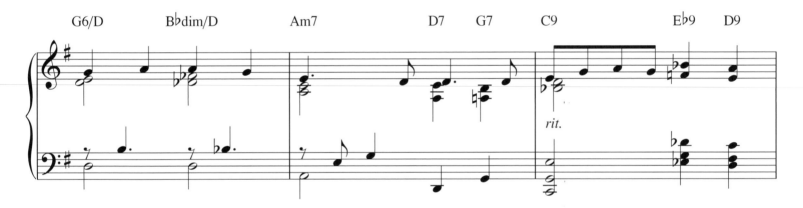

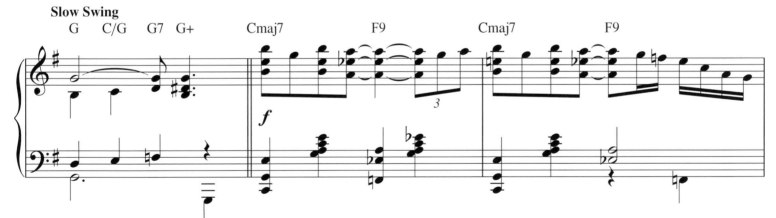

29

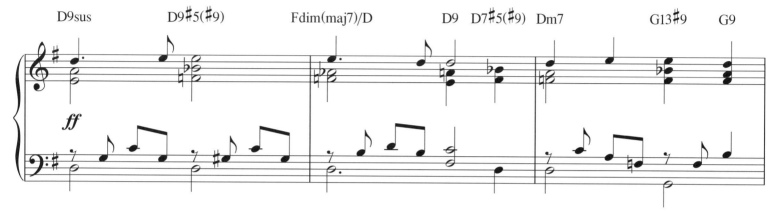

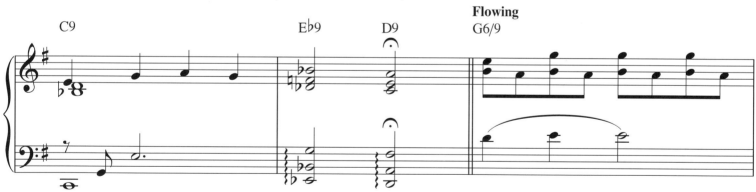

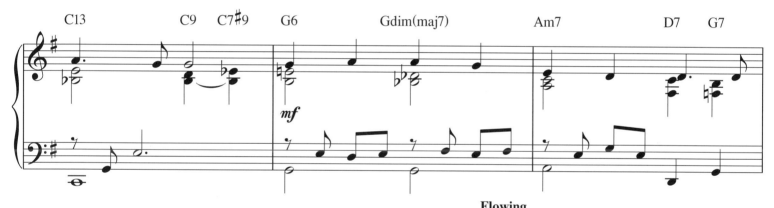

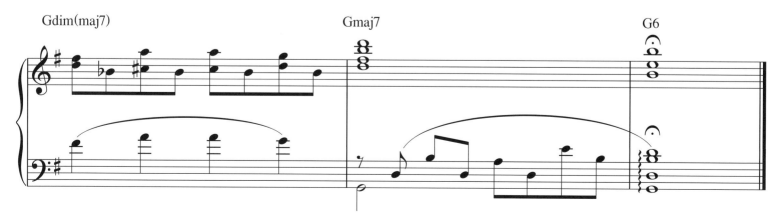

I GOT RHYTHM

Music and Lyrics by GEORGE GERSHWIN
and IRA GERSHWIN

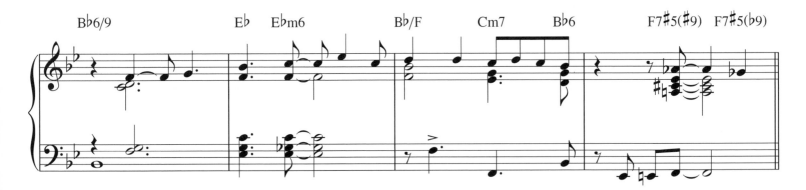

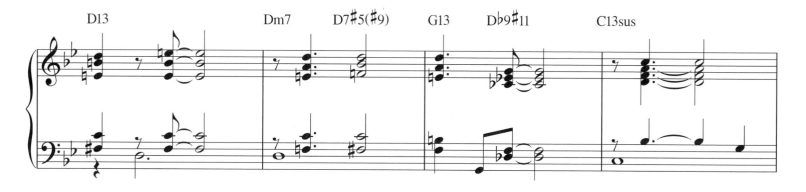

32

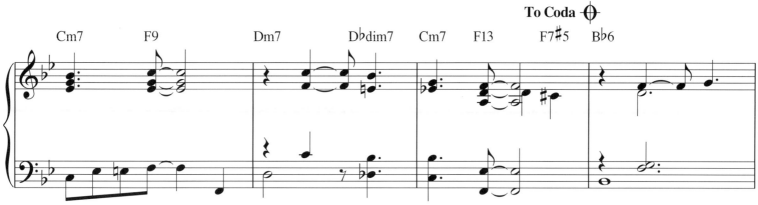

To Coda

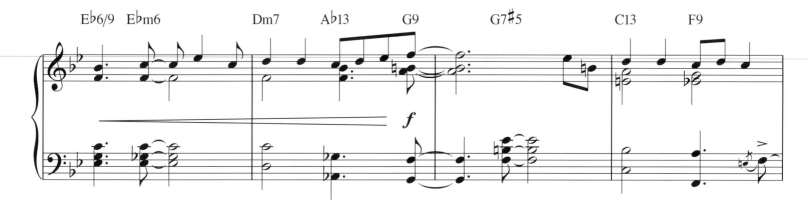

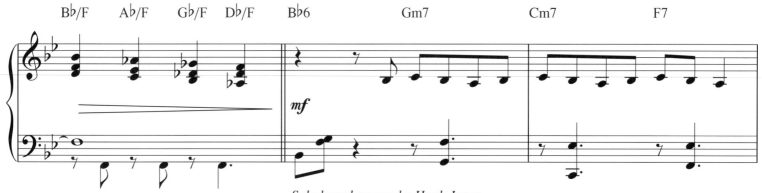

Solo based on one by Hank Jones

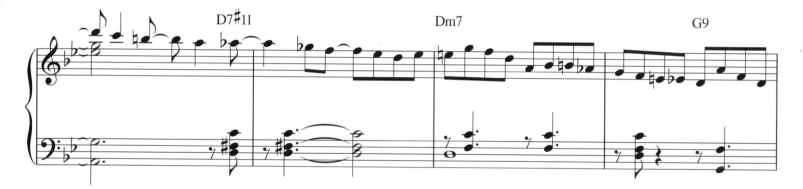

34

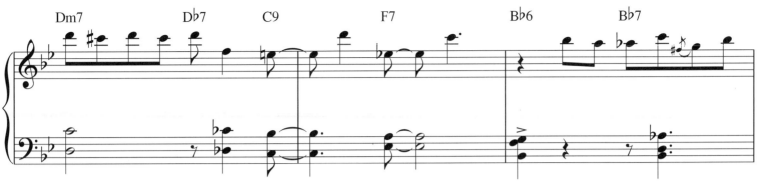

CODA

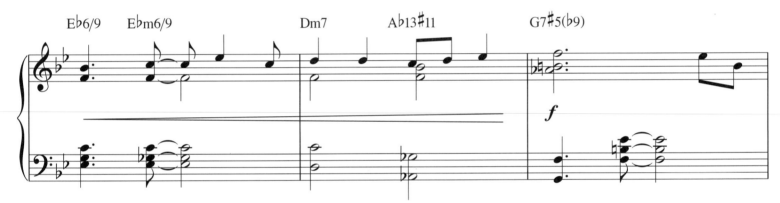

LET'S CALL THE WHOLE THING OFF

Music and Lyrics by GEORGE GERSHWIN
and IRA GERSHWIN

Moderate Swing

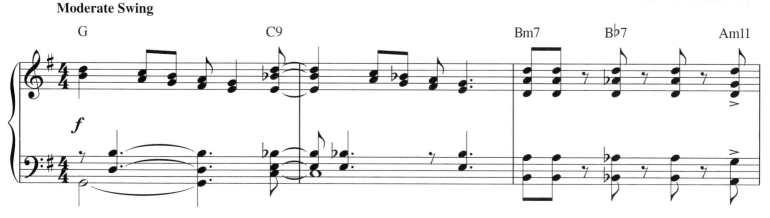

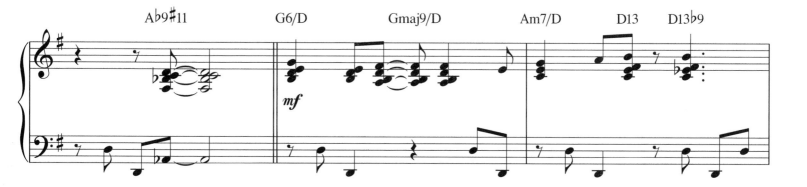

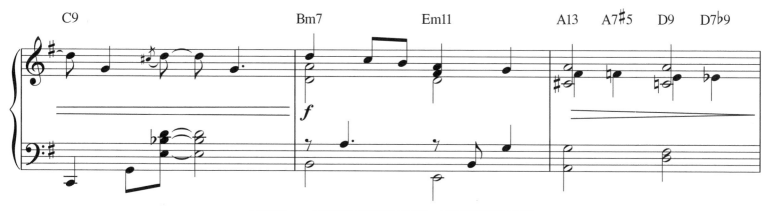

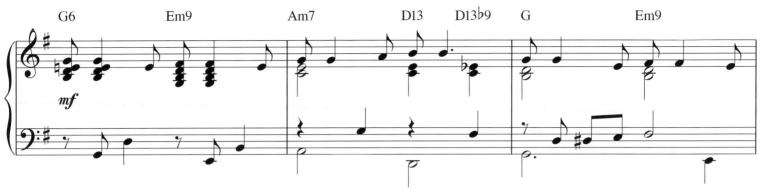

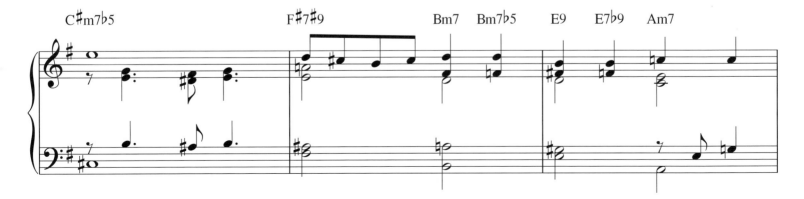

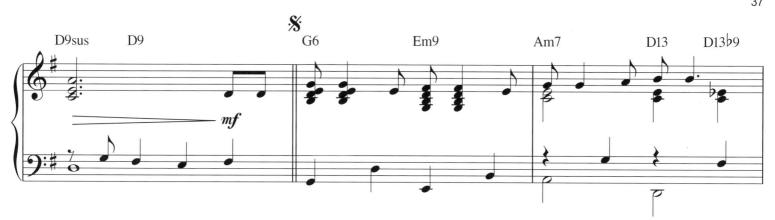

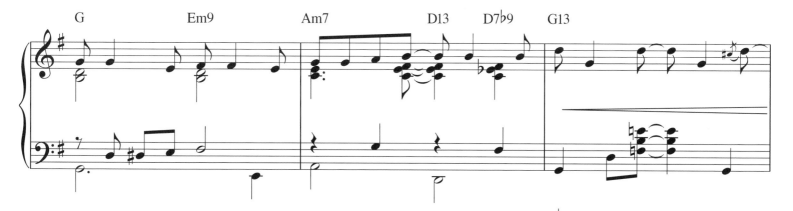

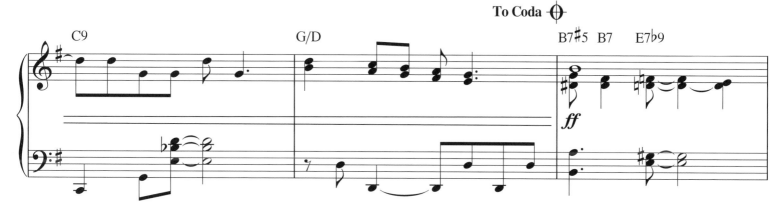

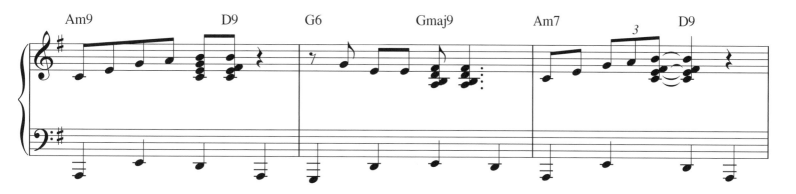

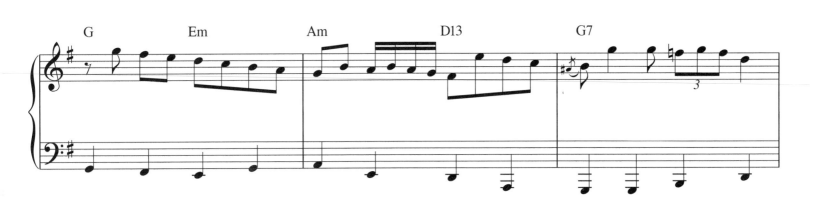

39

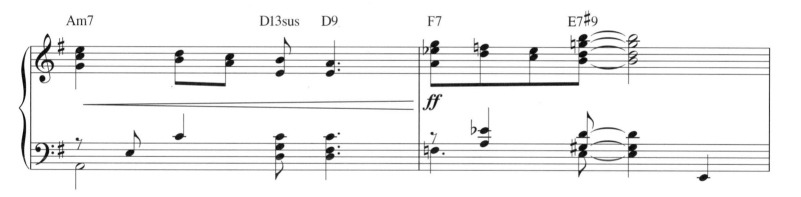

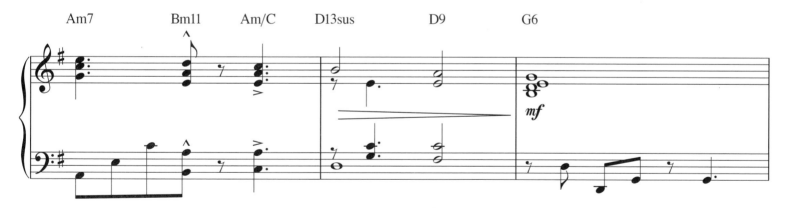

I LOVES YOU, PORGY

from PORGY AND BESS®

Music and Lyrics by GEORGE GERSHWIN,
DU BOSE and DOROTHY HEYWARD
and IRA GERSHWIN

Ballad

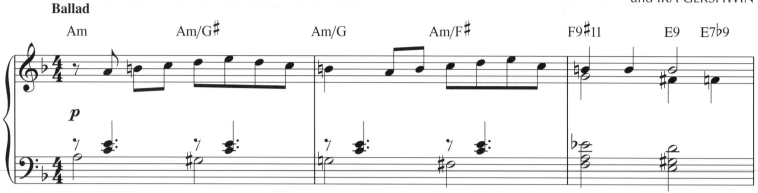

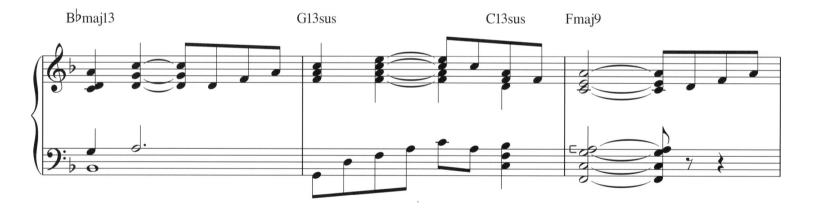

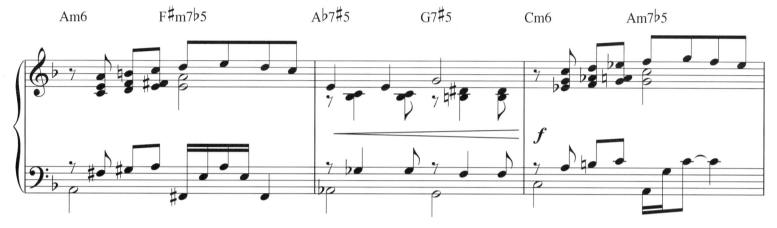

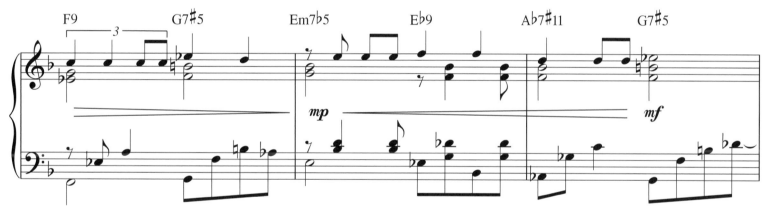

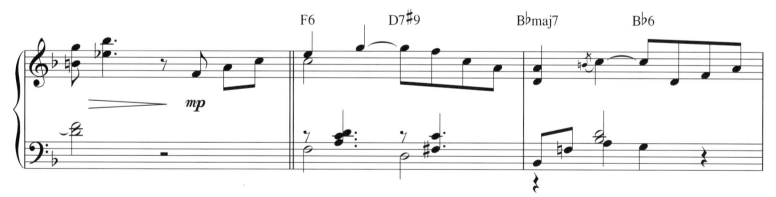

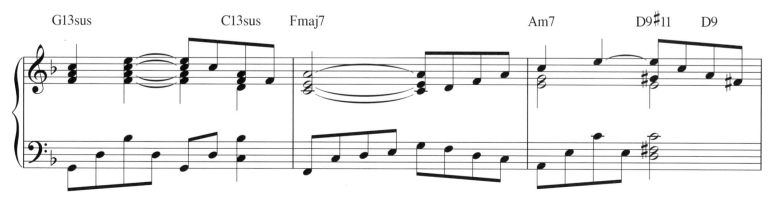

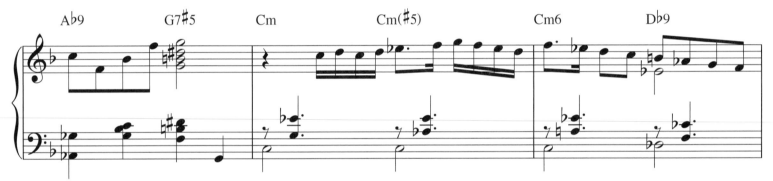

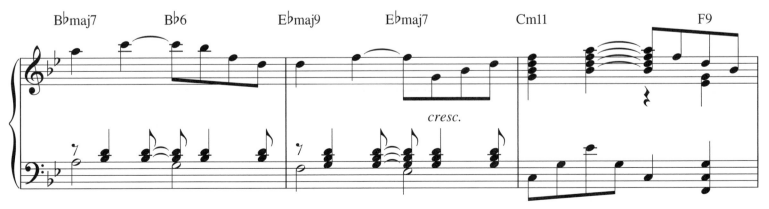

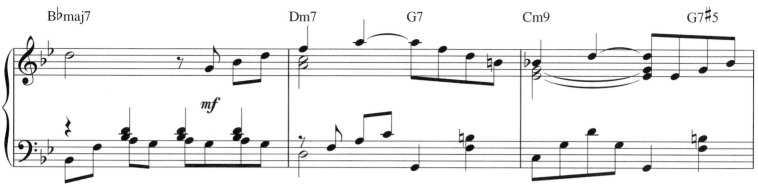

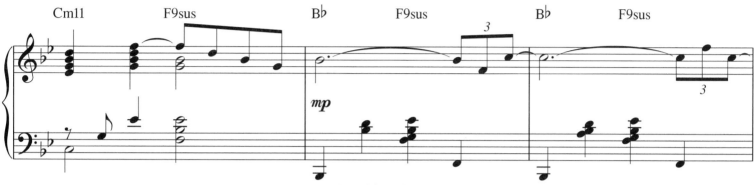

As played by Bill Evans on Peace Piece

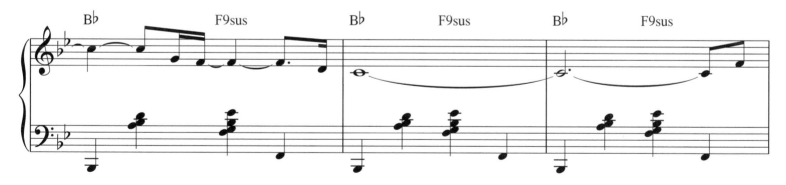

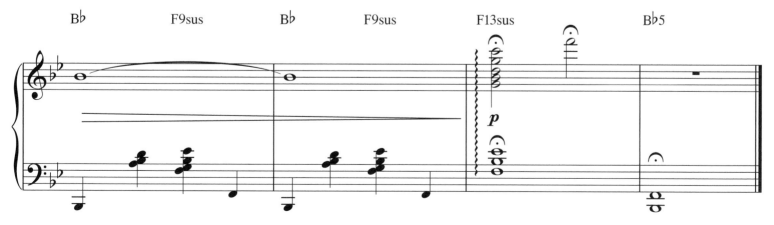

I'VE GOT A CRUSH ON YOU

Music and Lyrics by GEORGE GERSHWIN
and IRA GERSHWIN

Freely

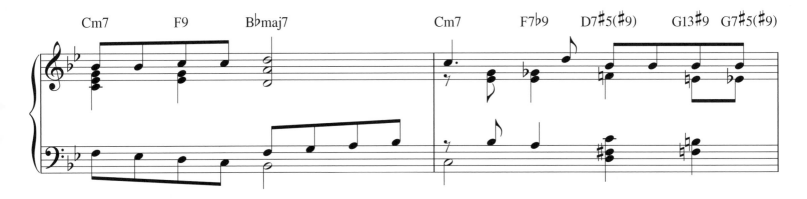

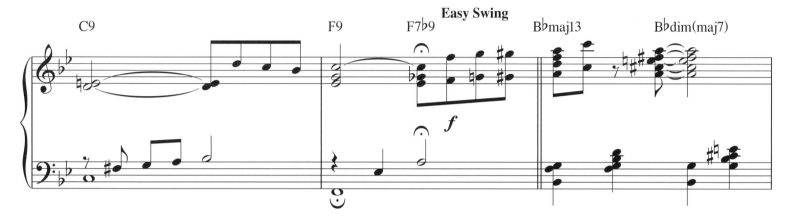

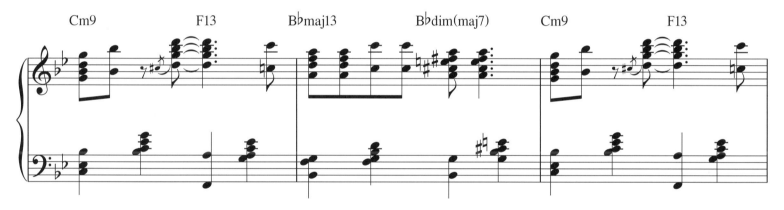

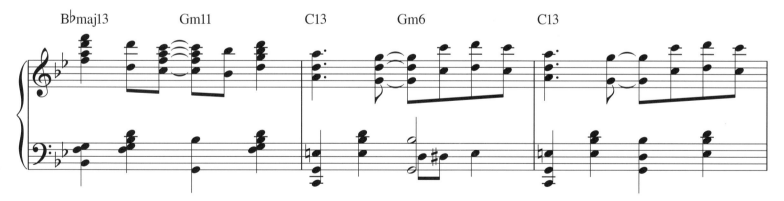

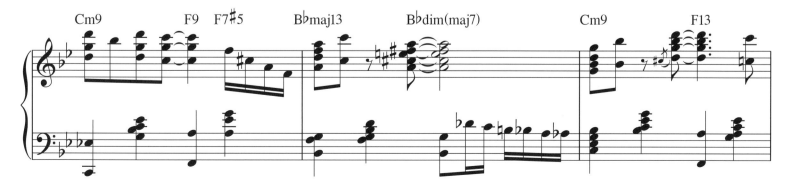

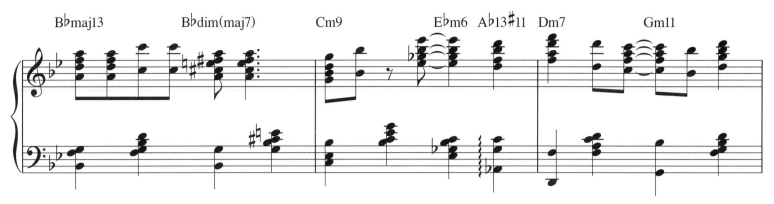

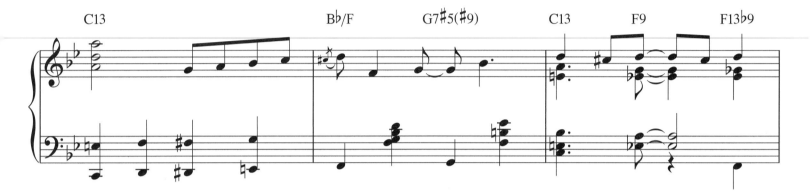

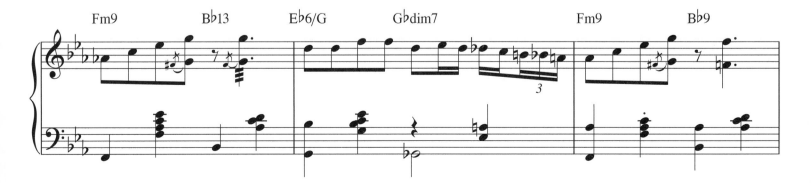

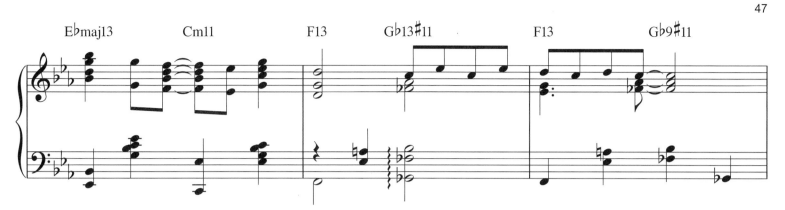

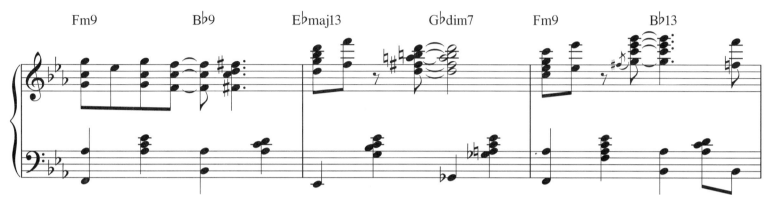

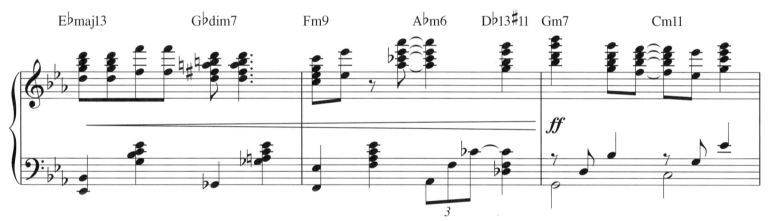

Slowly, straight 8ths

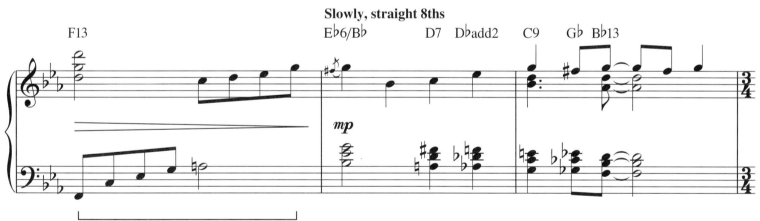

IT AIN'T NECESSARILY SO

from PORGY AND BESS®

Music and Lyrics by GEORGE GERSHWIN,
DU BOSE and DOROTHY HEYWARD
and IRA GERSHWIN

Moderately slow Swing

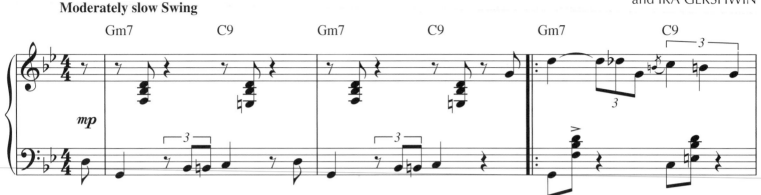

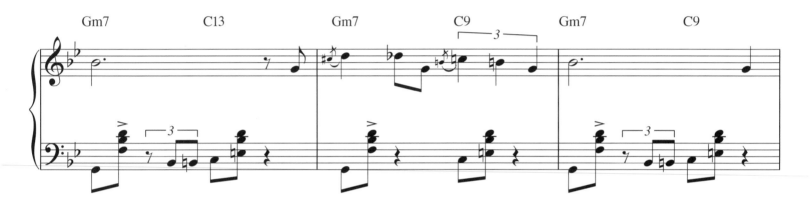

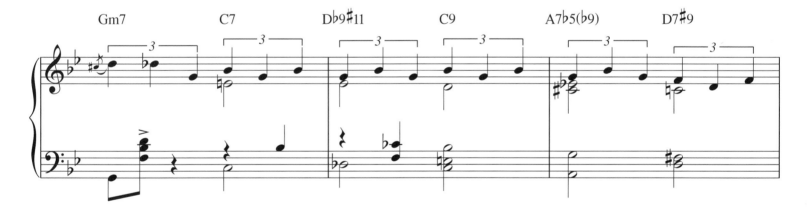

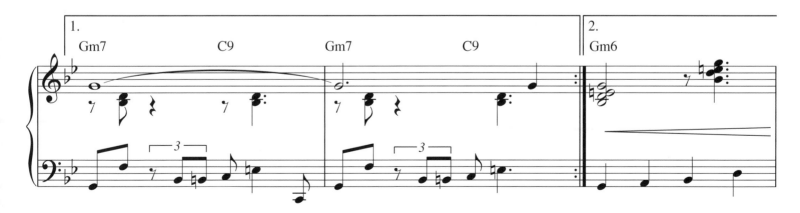

49

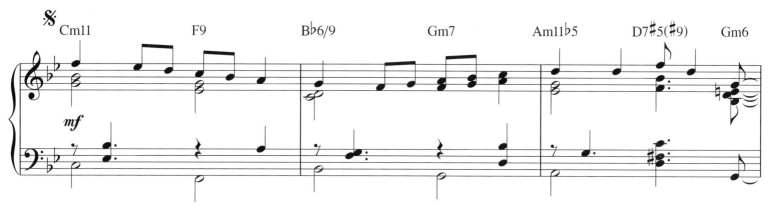

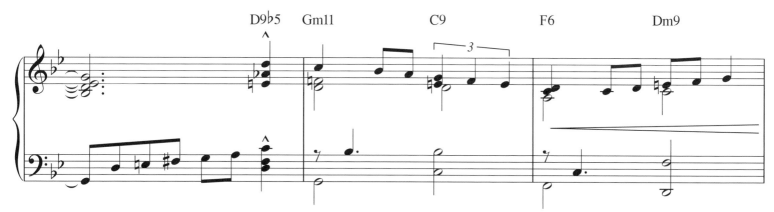

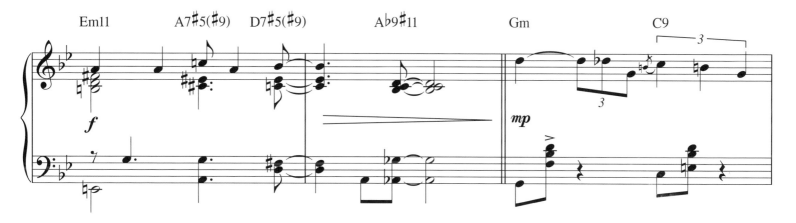

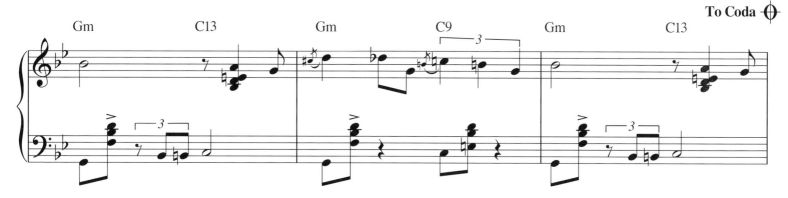

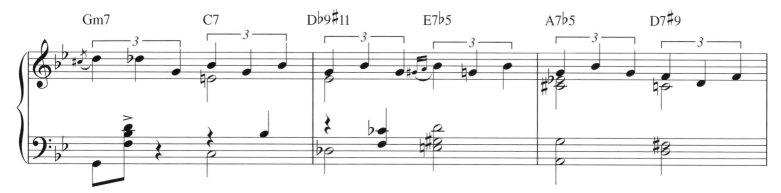

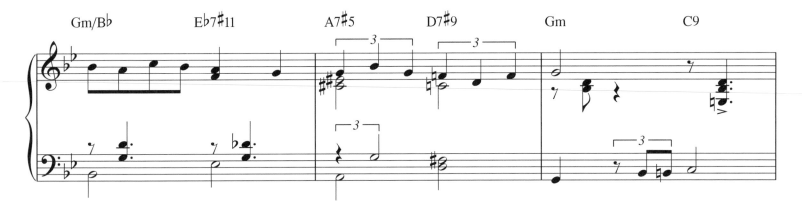

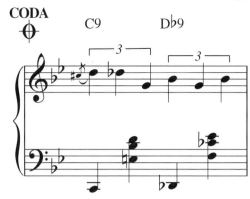
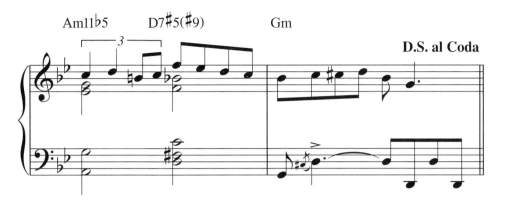
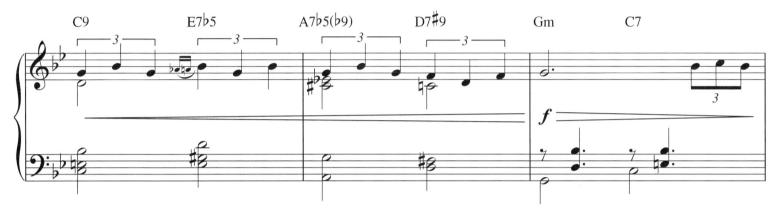
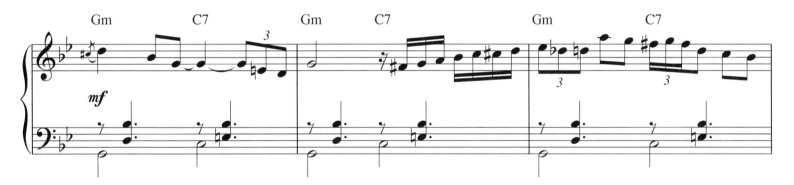
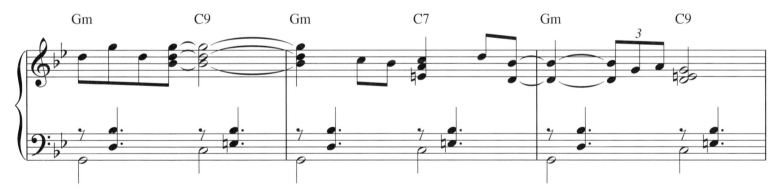
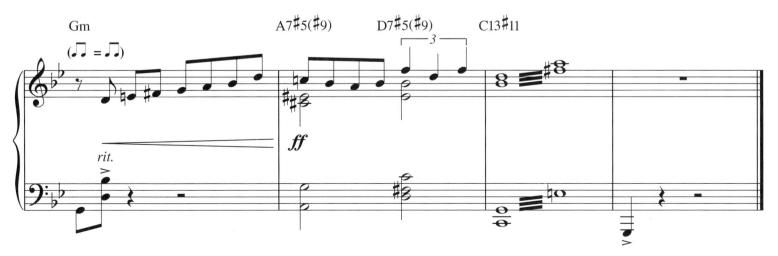

LOVE IS HERE TO STAY

Music and Lyrics by GEORGE GERSHWIN
and IRA GERSHWIN

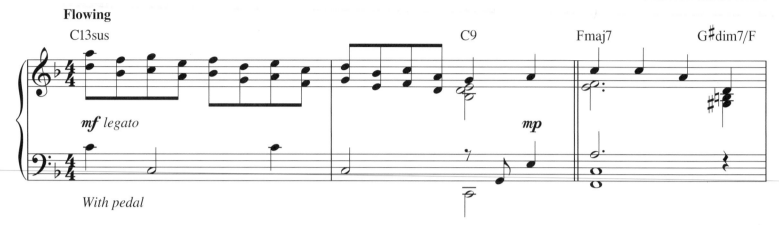

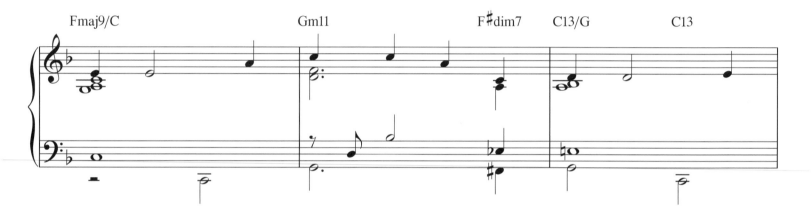

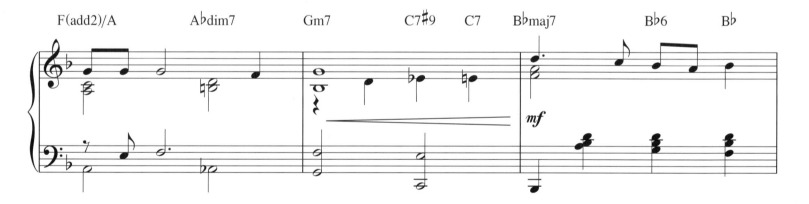

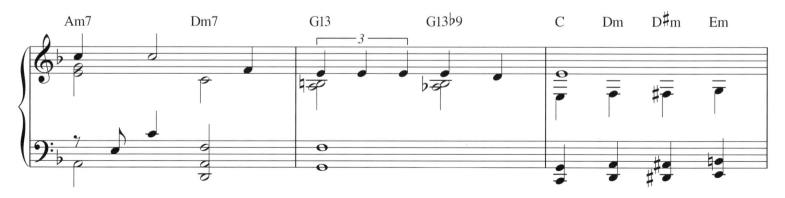

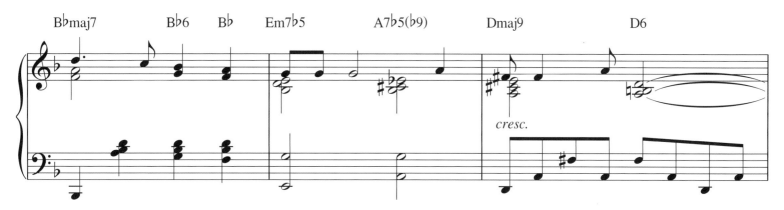

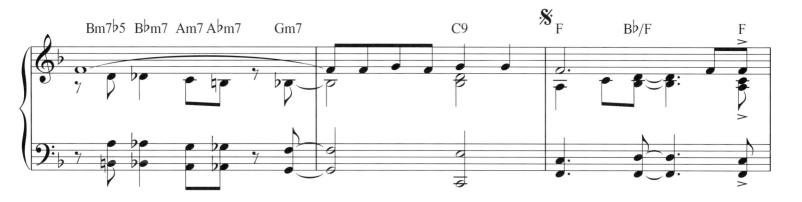

54

To Coda ⊕

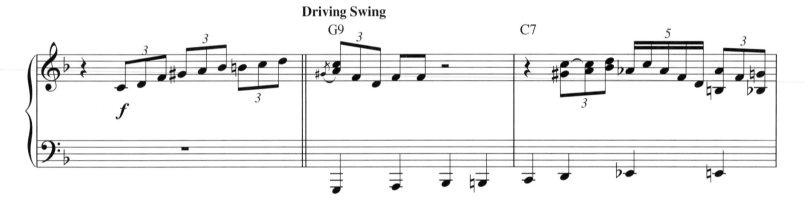

Driving Swing

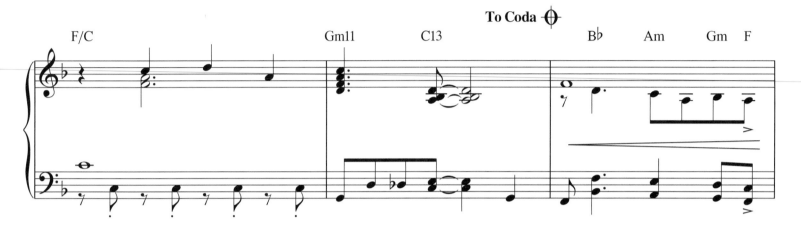

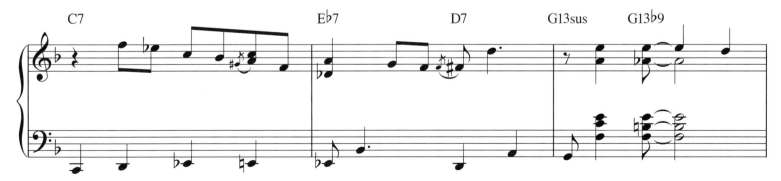

55

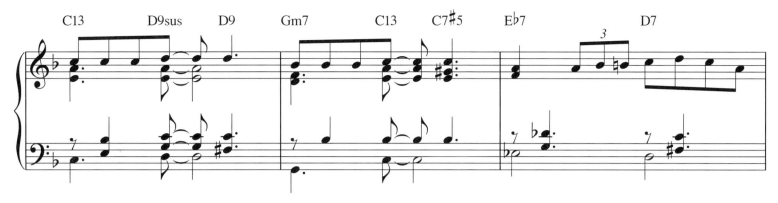

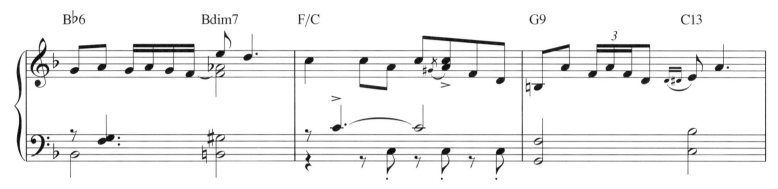

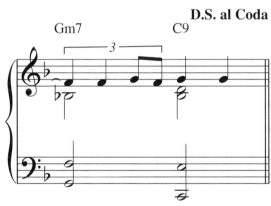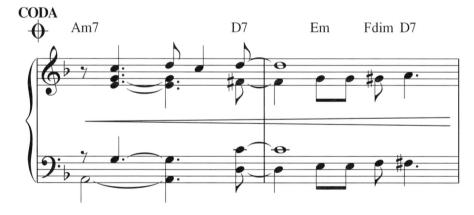

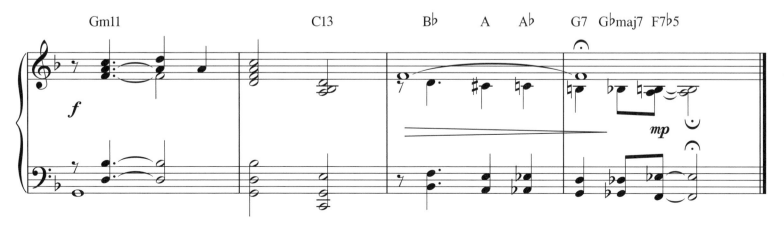

LOVE WALKED IN

Music and Lyrics by GEORGE GERSHWIN
and IRA GERSHWIN

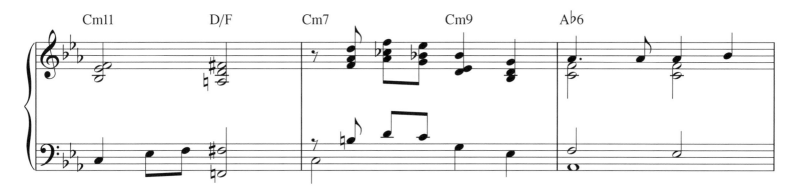

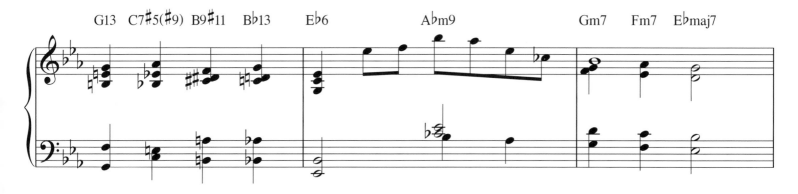

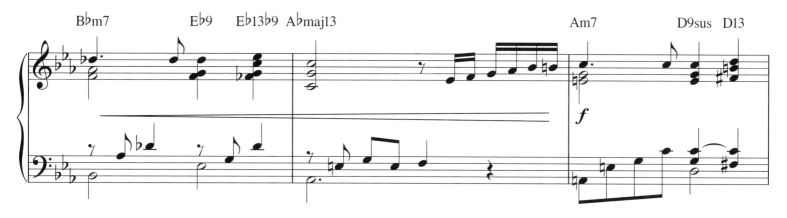

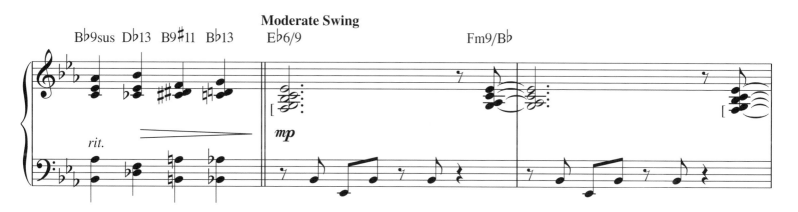

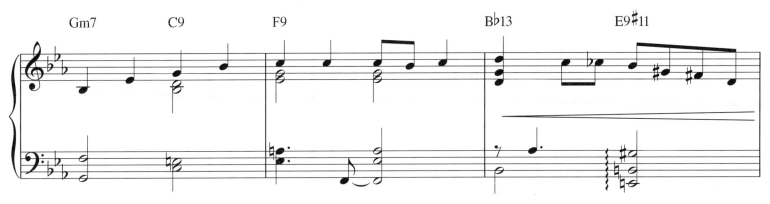

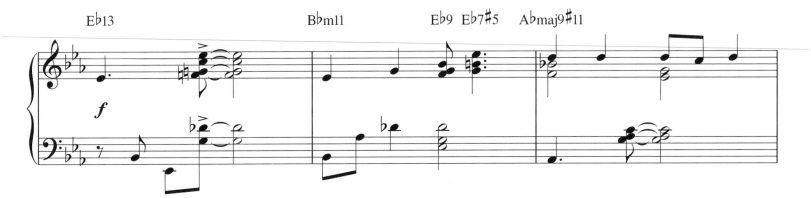

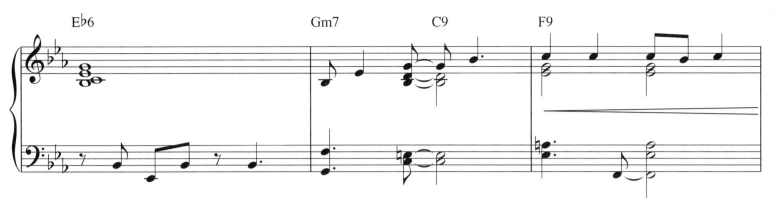

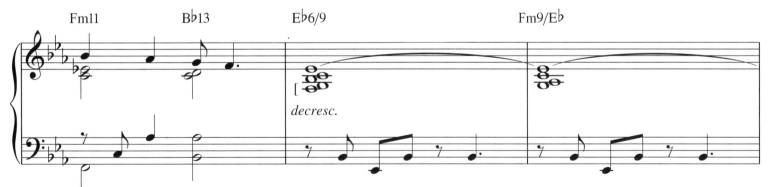

THE MAN I LOVE

Music and Lyrics by GEORGE GERSHWIN
and IRA GERSHWIN

Moderately slow, with rubato

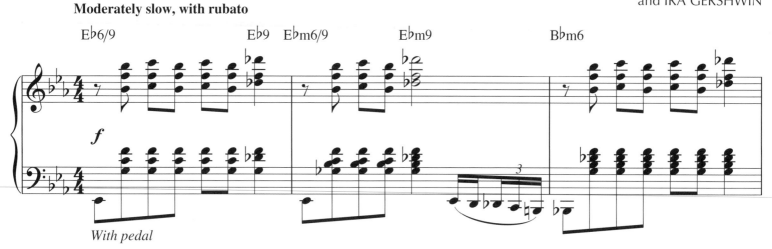

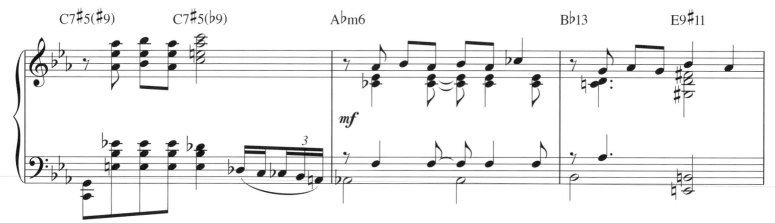

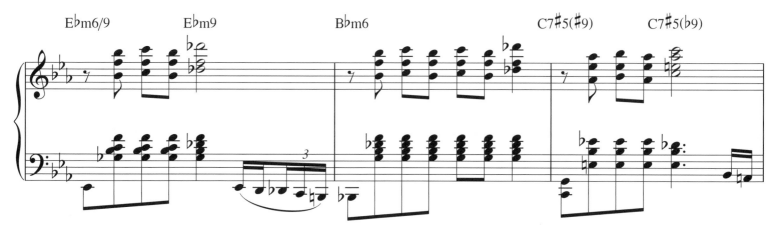

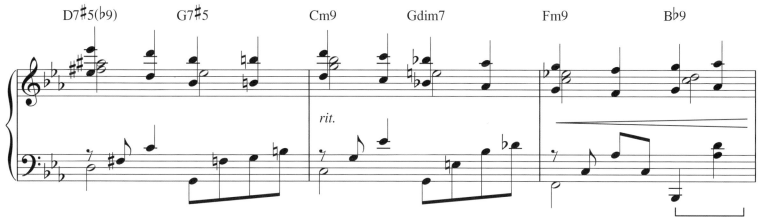

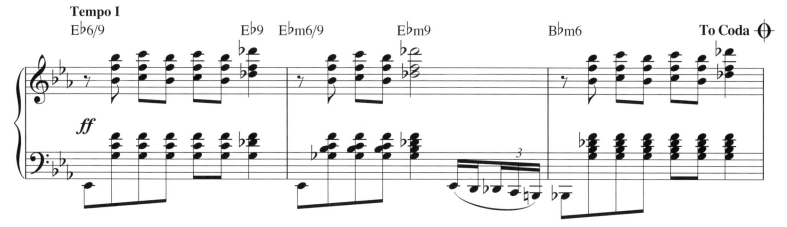

62

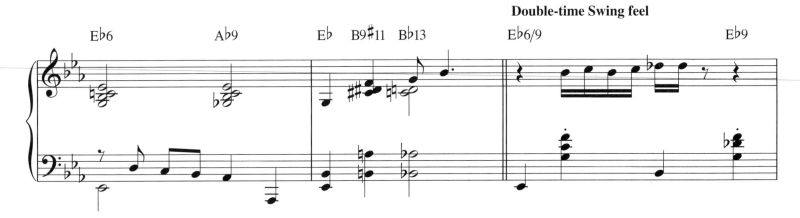

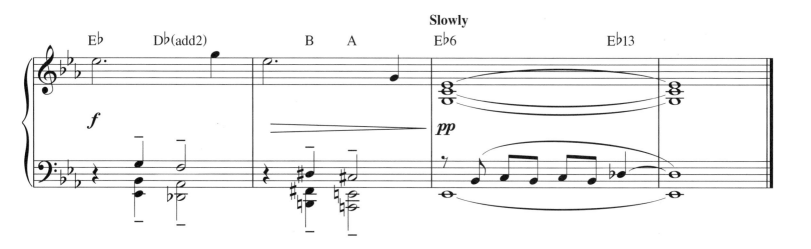

NICE WORK IF YOU CAN GET IT

Music and Lyrics by GEORGE GERSHWIN
and IRA GERSHWIN

Bright Swing

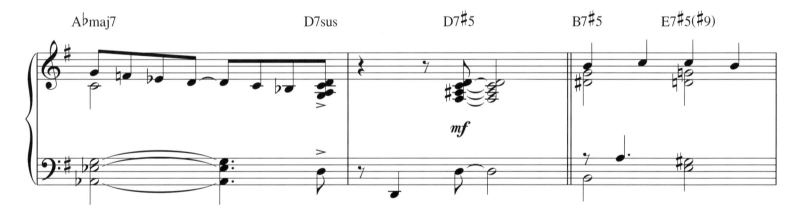

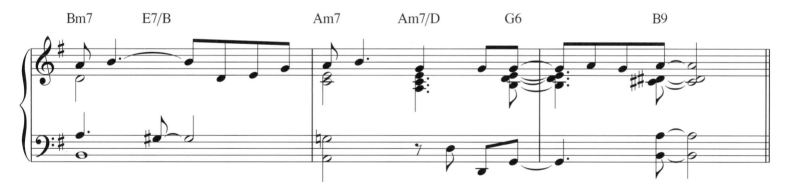

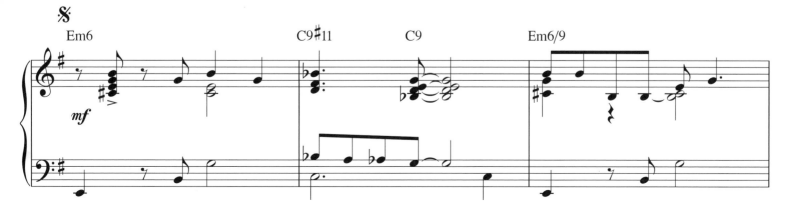

To Coda ⊕

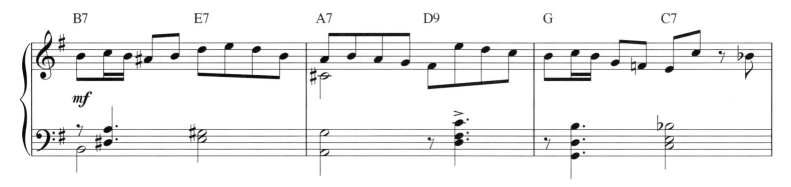

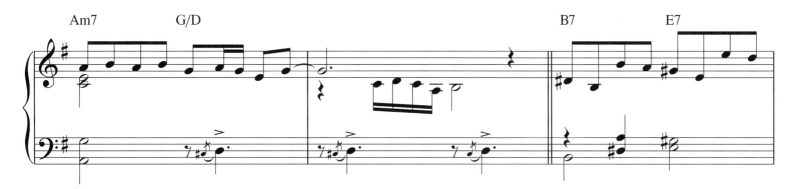

D.S. al Coda

CODA

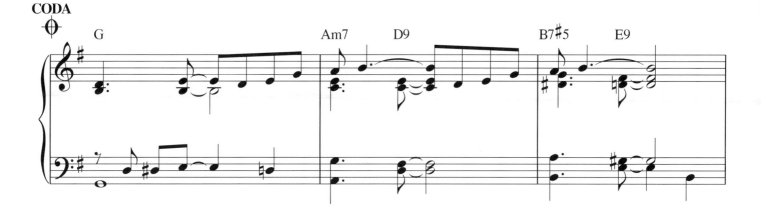

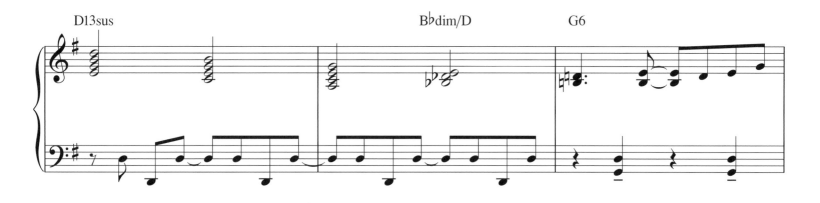

SOMEBODY LOVES ME

Music by GEORGE GERSHWIN
Lyrics by B.G. DeSYLVA and BALLARD MacDONALD

Moderate Swing

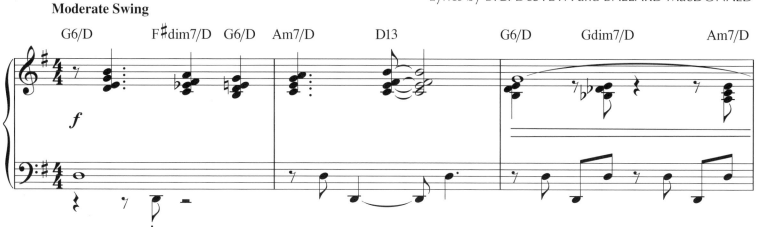

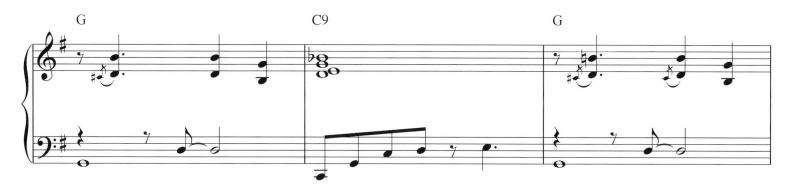

70

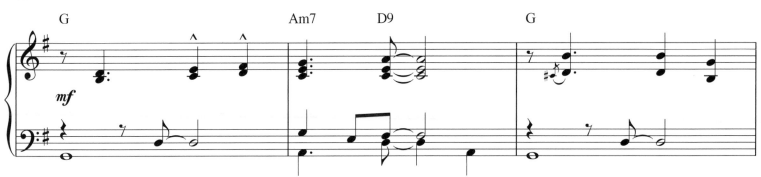

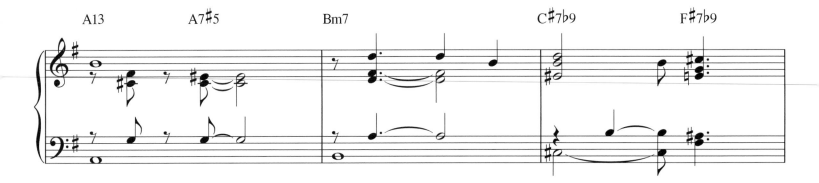

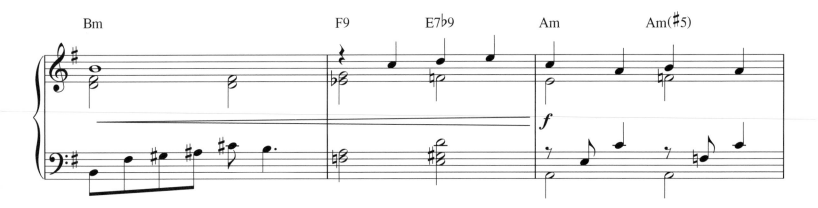

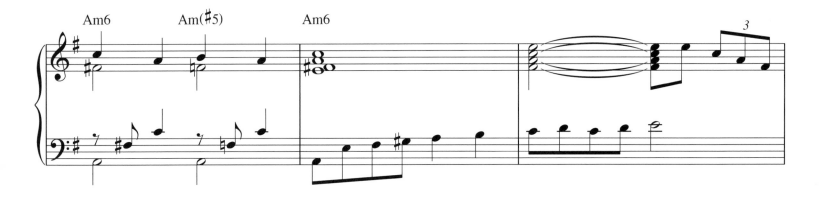

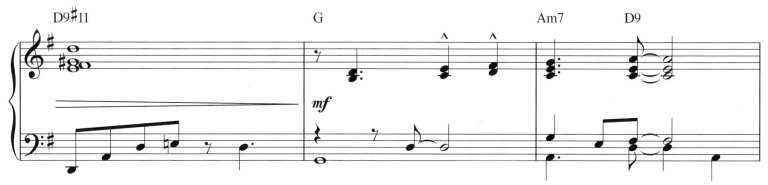
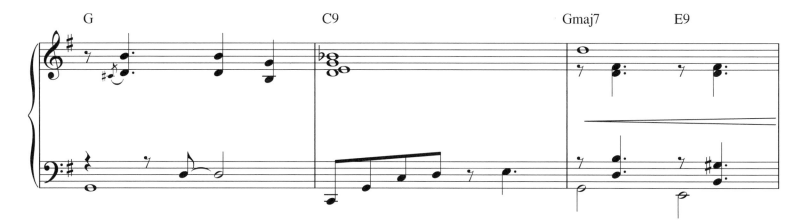
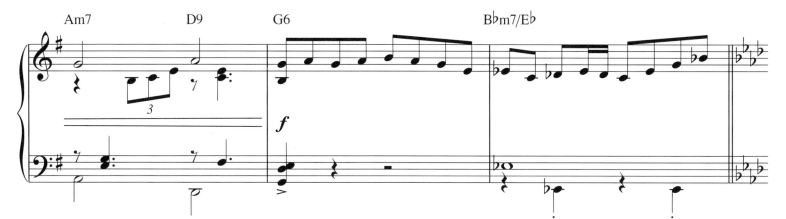
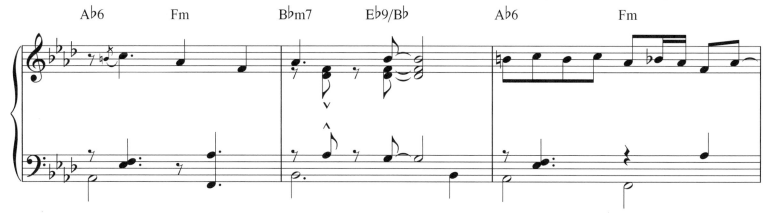

72

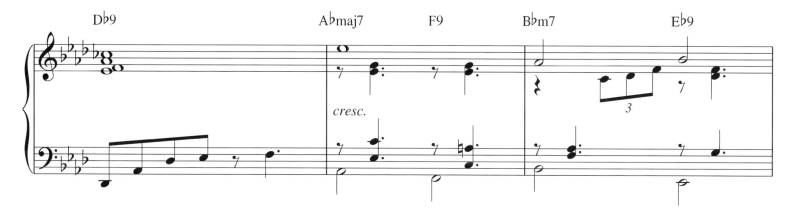

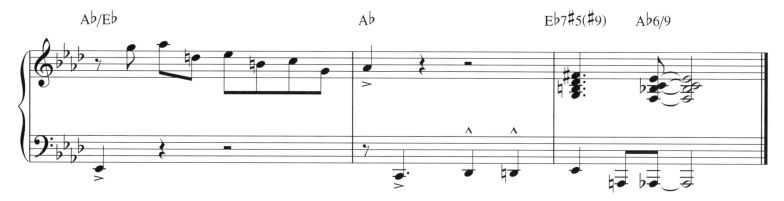

OH, LADY BE GOOD!

Music and Lyrics by GEORGE GERSHWIN
and IRA GERSHWIN

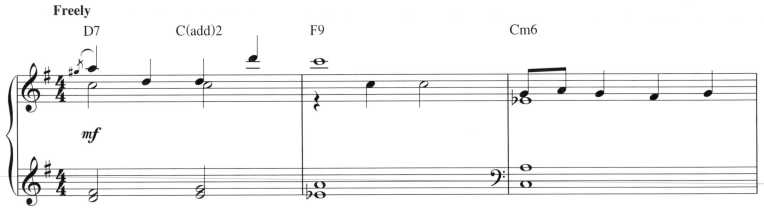

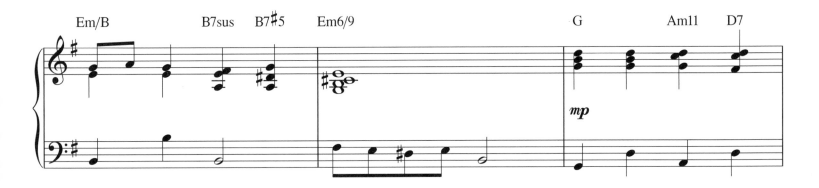

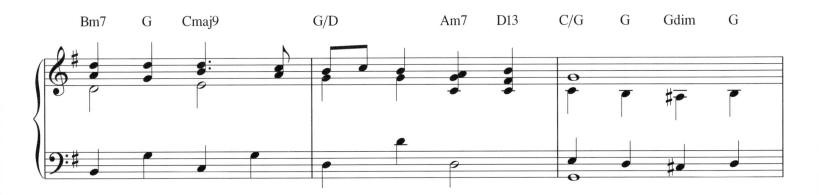

Flowing

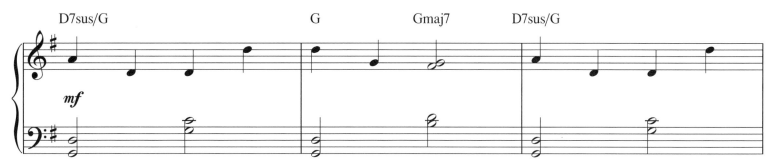

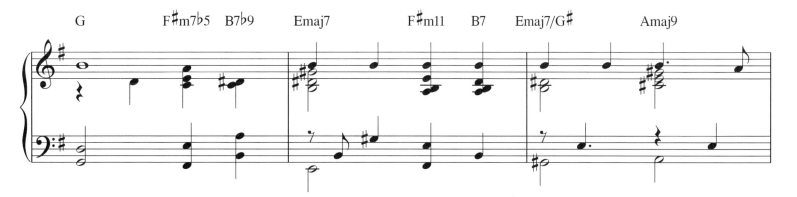

Fast Swing

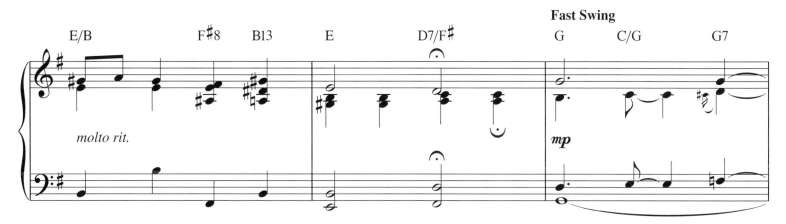

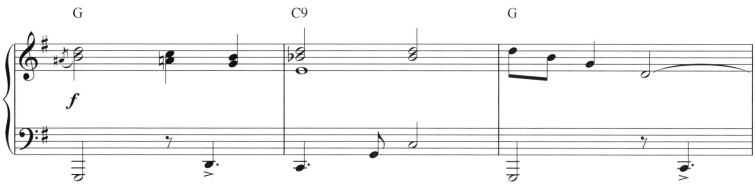

76

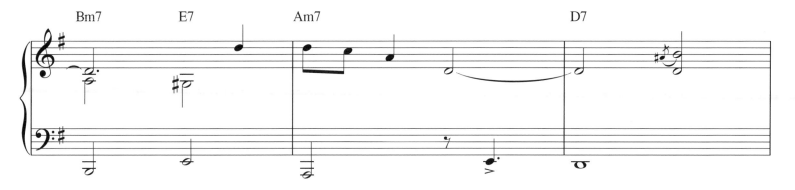

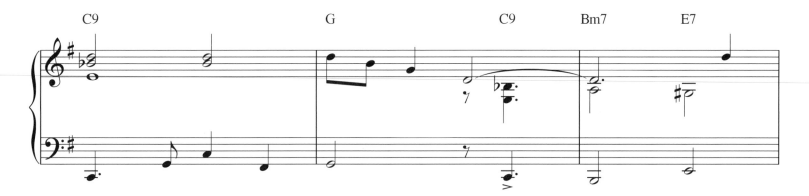

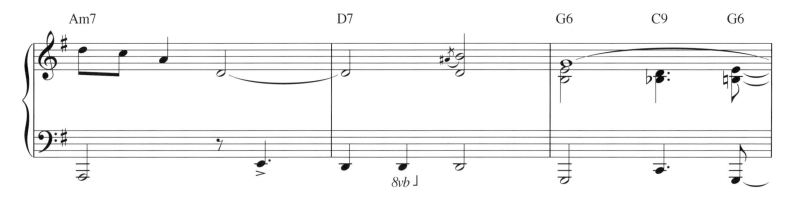

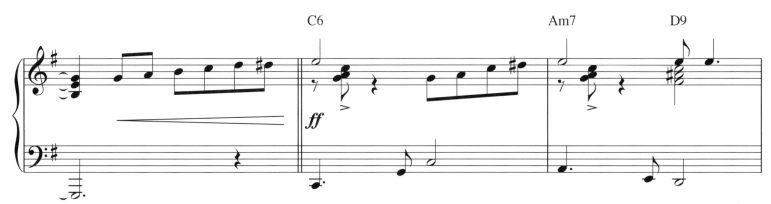

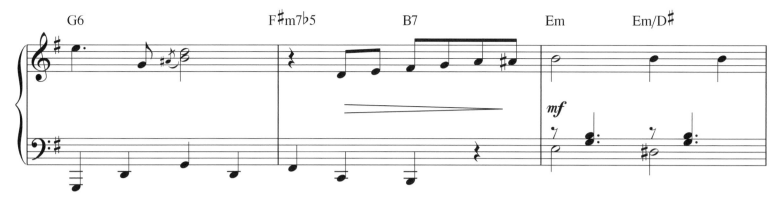

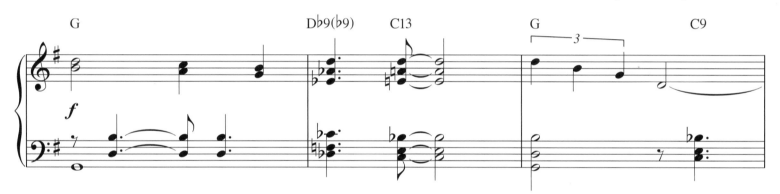

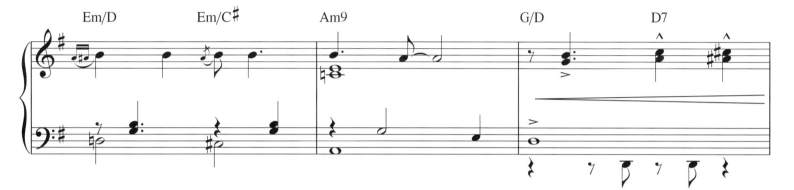

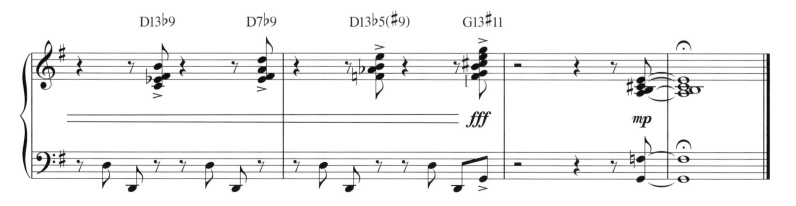

'S WONDERFUL

Music and Lyrics by GEORGE GERSHWIN
and IRA GERSHWIN

Bright Swing

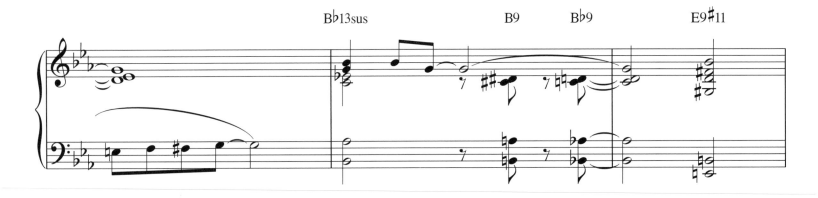

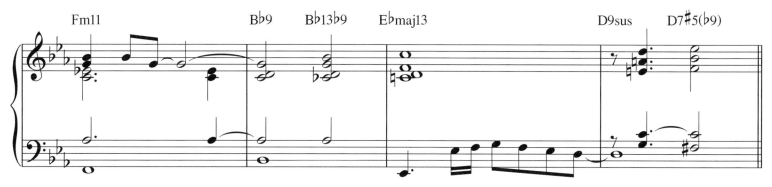

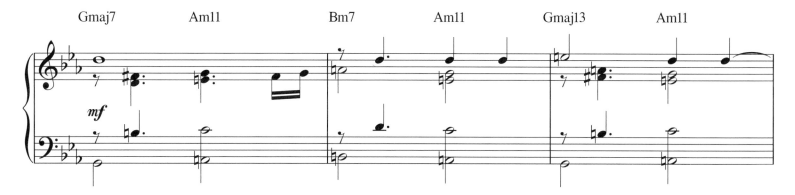

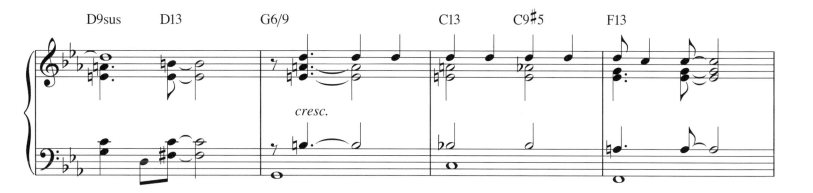

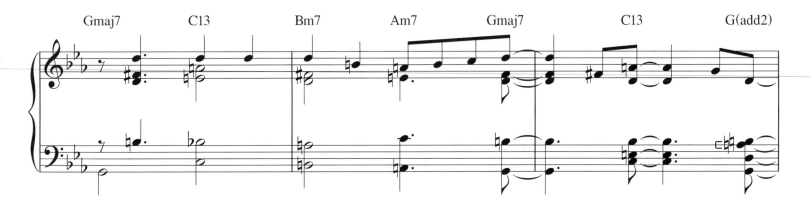

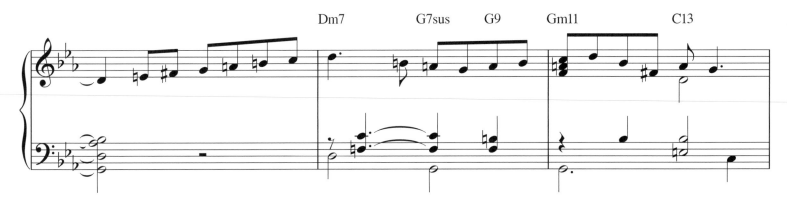

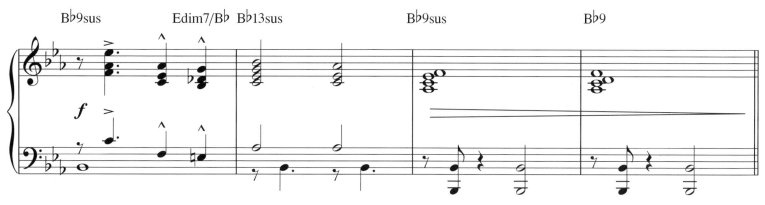

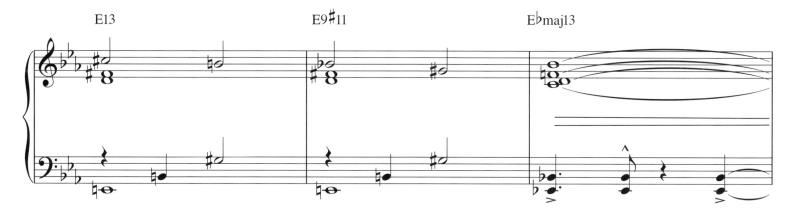

SOMEONE TO WATCH OVER ME

Music and Lyrics by GEORGE GERSHWIN
and IRA GERSHWIN

Freely, with rubato

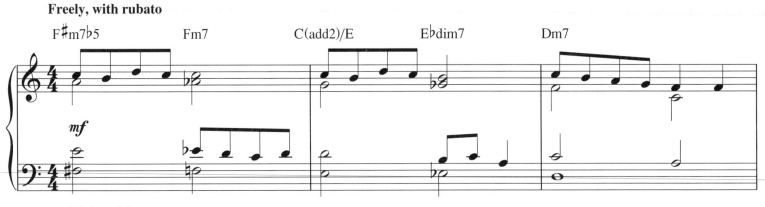

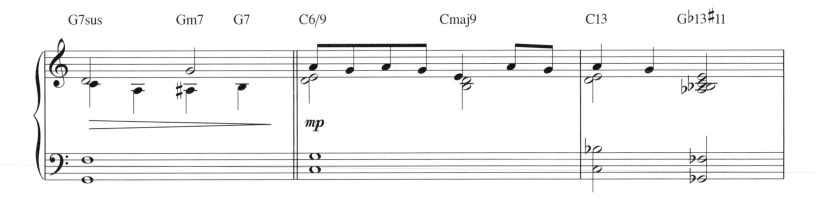

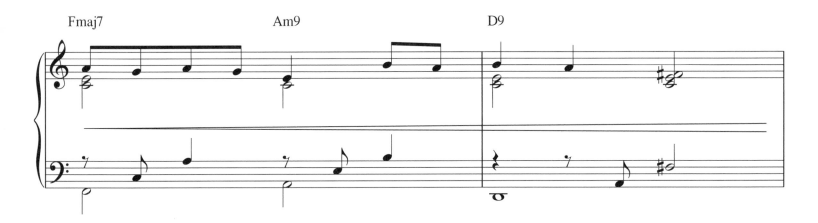

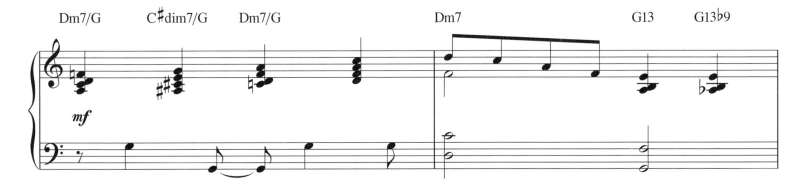

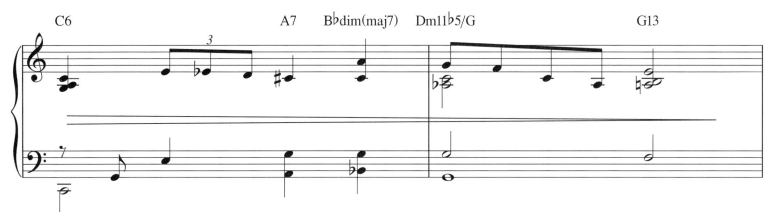

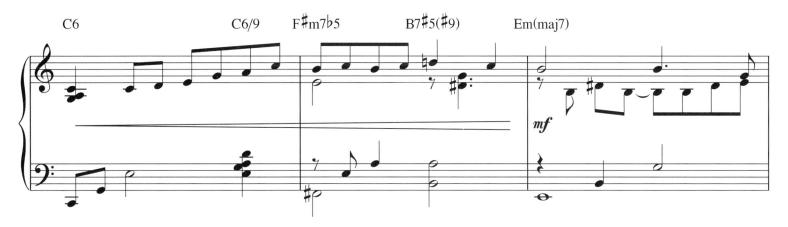

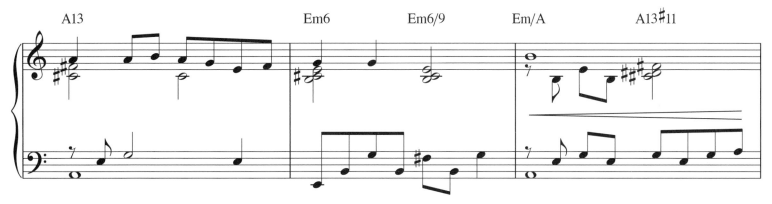

84

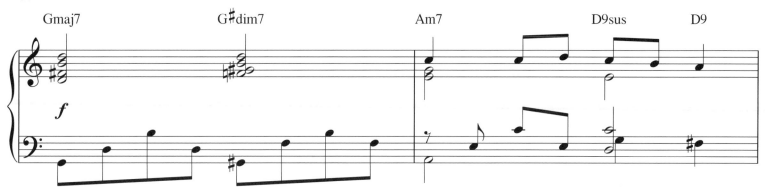

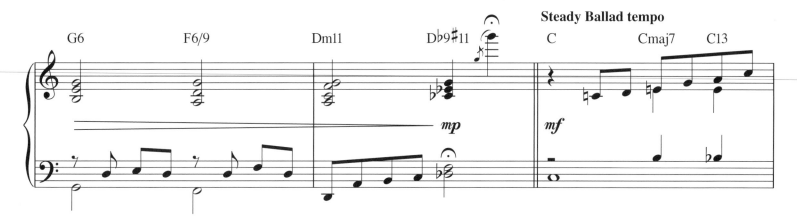

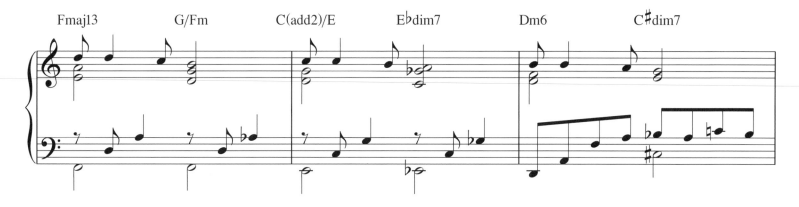

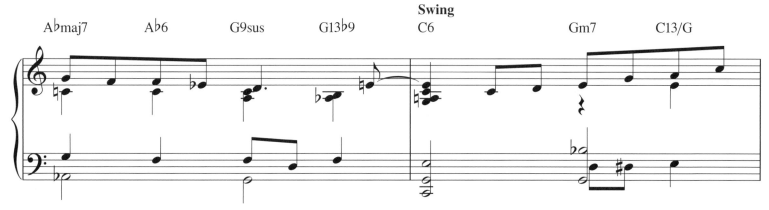

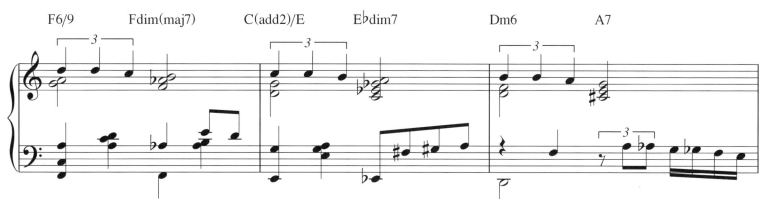

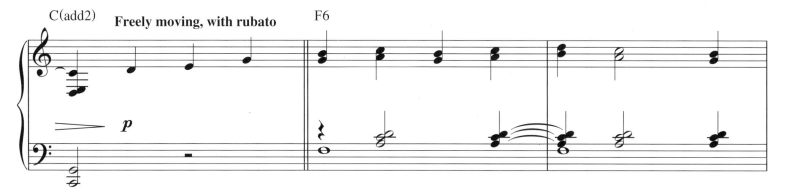

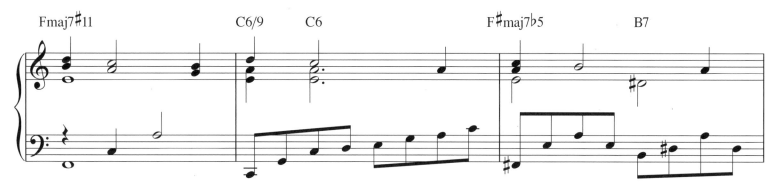

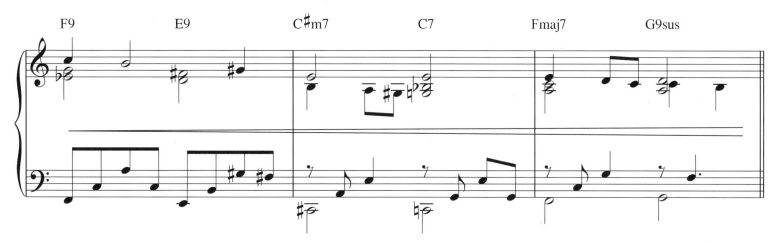

Steady ballad tempo

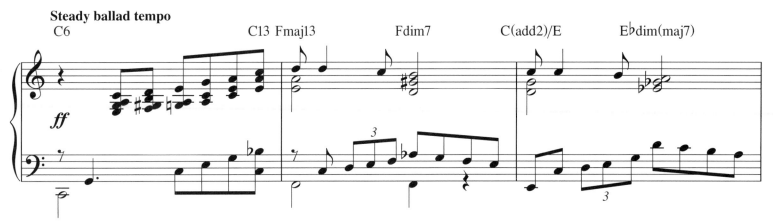

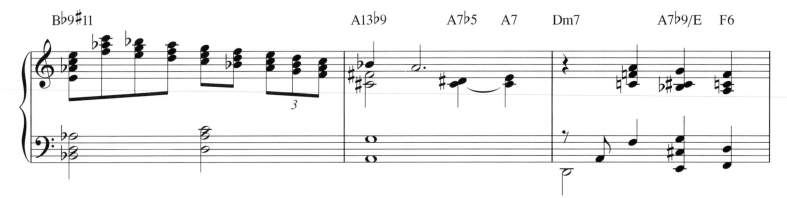

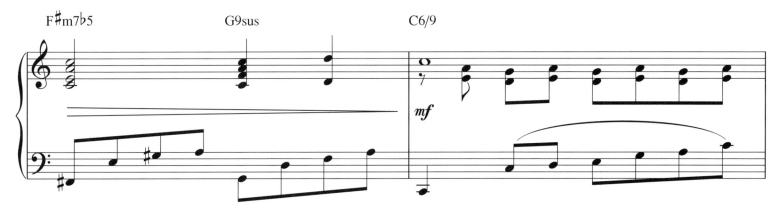

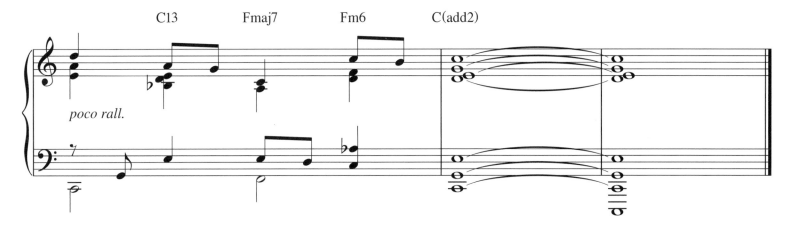

SUMMERTIME
from PORGY AND BESS®

Music and Lyrics by GEORGE GERSHWIN,
DU BOSE and DOROTHY HEYWARD
and IRA GERSHWIN

Languorous Swing, with expression

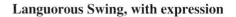

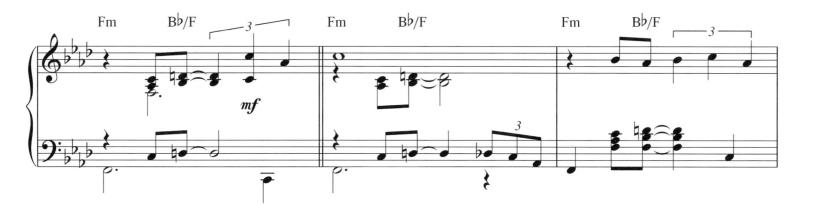

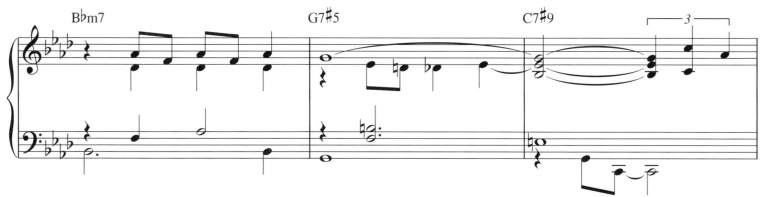

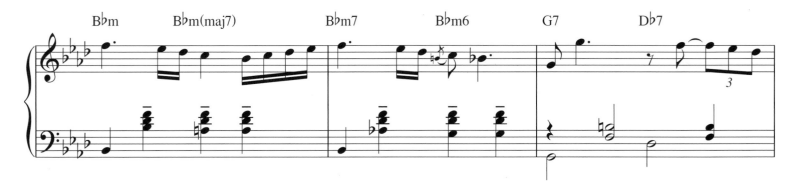

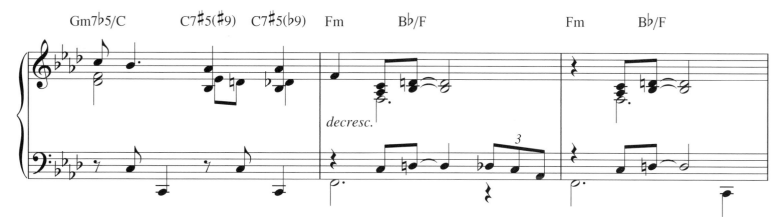

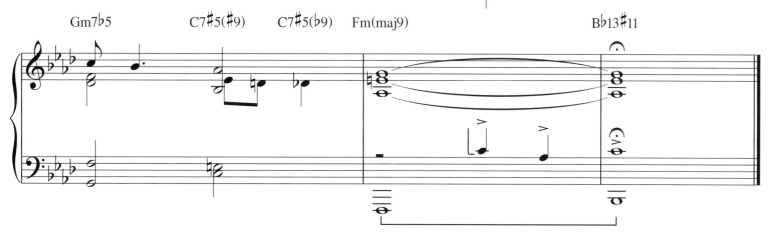

THEY CAN'T TAKE THAT AWAY FROM ME

Music and Lyrics by GEORGE GERSHWIN
and IRA GERSHWIN

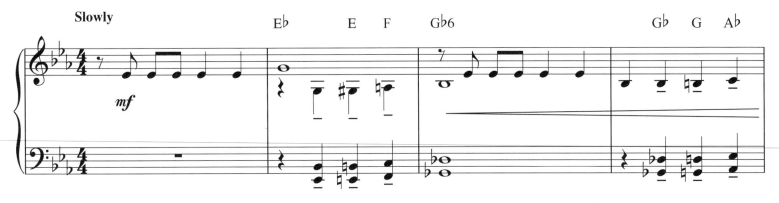

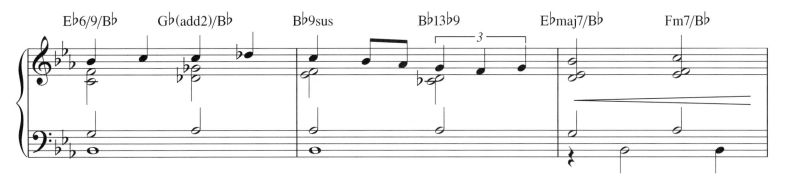

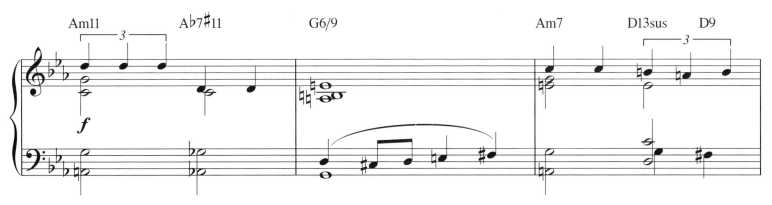

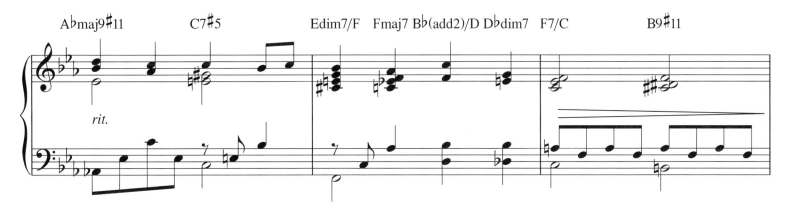

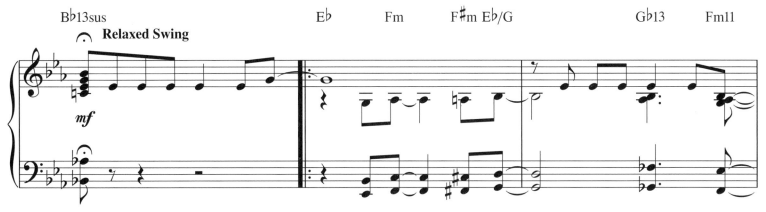

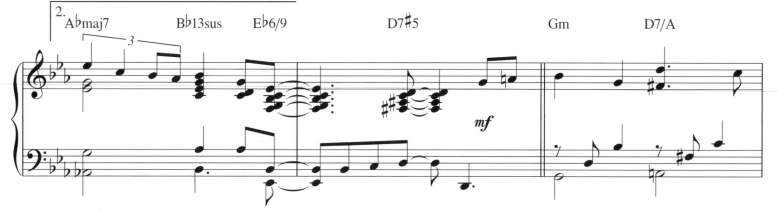

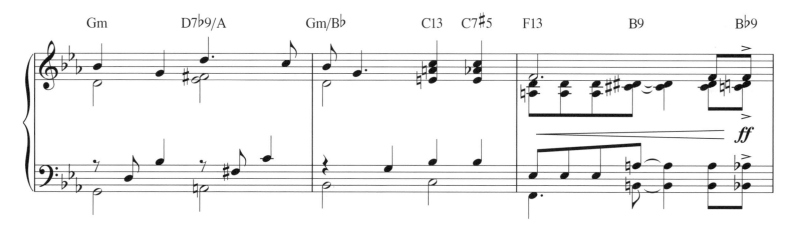

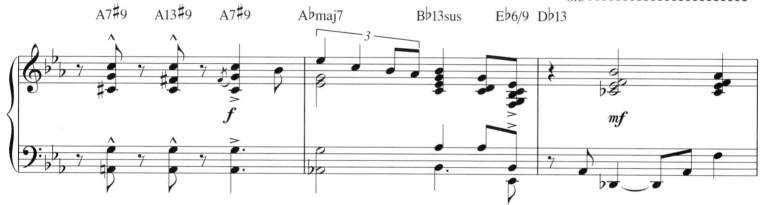

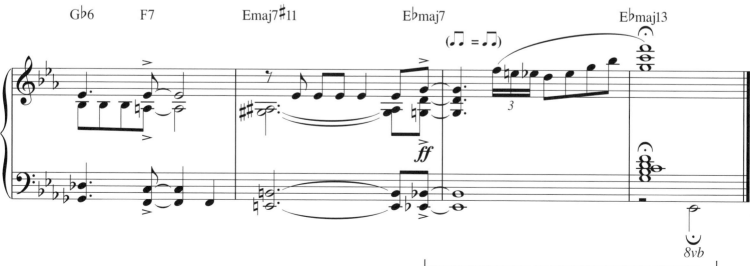

THEY ALL LAUGHED

Music and Lyrics by GEORGE GERSHWIN
and IRA GERSHWIN

Medium Swing

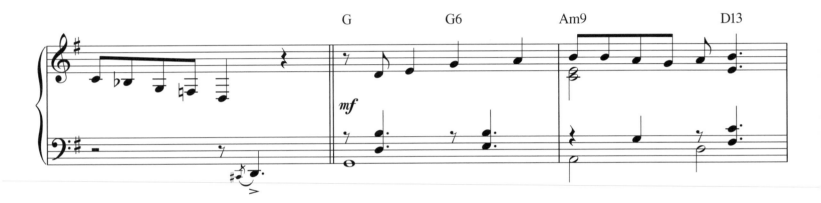

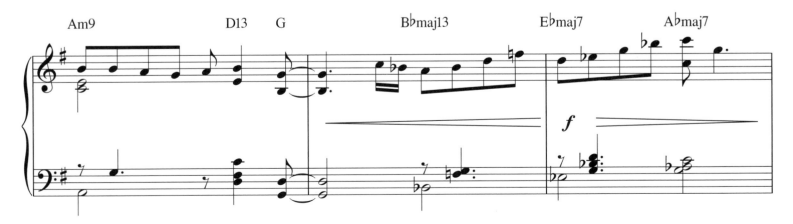

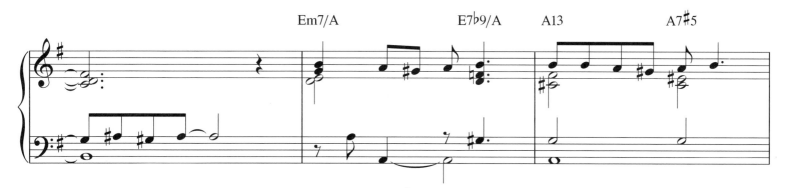

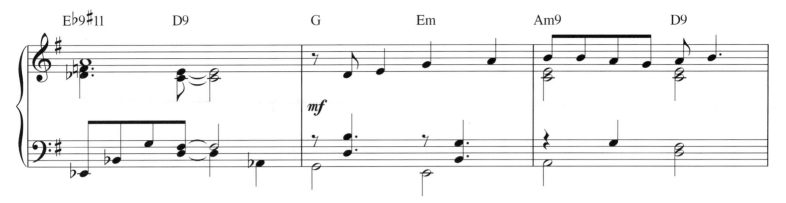

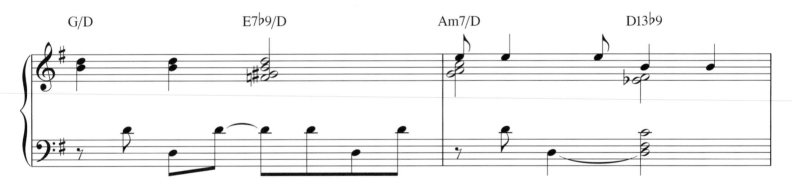

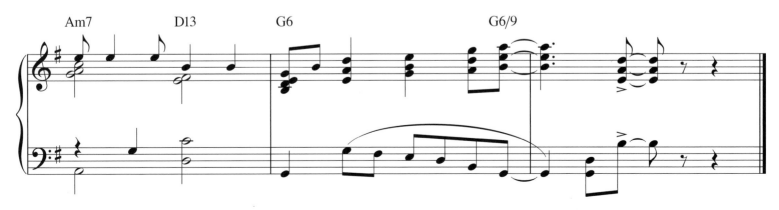